SO YOU WANT TO OPEN A DAY CARE CENTER.....
A BASIC "HOW TO DO IT" GUIDE

by

Patricia C. Gallagher

ISBN #0-943135-05-2
Library of Congress #87-82026

P.C. Gallagher
Child Care Consultants
301 Holly Hill Road
Richboro, PA 18954
215-364-1945

AVAILABLE MAIL ORDER ONLY!

These informative books are also made available to send as a "gift" to the person of your choice. Simply mark your order "GIFT" and a card and selected book will be mailed to the designated address signed with your name and best wishes.

"CHILD CARE AND YOU"
HOW TO START A PROFITABLE DAY CARE PROGRAM IN THE HOME

This comprehensive guide to organizing a profitable Home Based Day Care business is invaluable for setting up a successful program. Everything that you need to get started is included. Licensing, Insurance, Zoning, Arts & Crafts, Safety Tips, Emergency Procedures, etc. are discussed. You can start you own program within a few weeks. ($19.95)

SO YOU WANT TO OPEN A DAY CARE CENTER.....
(Within A Corporation, Hospital, Nursing Home, College or Outside Facility)

For Teachers, Nurses, Corporate Personnel, Hospital Staff, College Students, and anyone who asks "How Do I Get Started?" This manual will provide vital information on: Where To Begin; Guiding Principles; Developmental Needs, Educational Plans Activities; Suggested Equipment and Supplies; Program Cautions (Potential problems and how to avoid them); Tips From Experienced Directors; Free Information Resources...and much more!! ($12.95)

ROBIN'S PLAY & LEARN BOOK
HOW TO ENTERTAIN CHILDREN AT HOME OR IN PRESCHOOL

Preschool Teachers, Parents, Early Childhood Students, Babysitters, Grandparents, Scout Leaders, Student Teachers will appreciate the hundreds of ideas for: Simple Crafts, Games, No-Bake Cooking Recipes, Field Trip Ideas, Songs, Finger-Plays and Learning Activities. The book is chock full of creative ideas. It will show you what to do when a child exclaims, "But there's nothing to do!" ($9.95)

To order, please send check or money order to P.C. Gallagher at the above address, and include $2.00 per order for postage and handling.

Name_____

Address_____

City_____ State_____ Zip_____

Number of Books Ordered_____ Amount Enclosed_____

If you order twelve copies or more, discount price is available!

<u>DISCOUNT PRICE LIST</u>
Prices Effective December 1, 1987

1. <u>CHILD CARE AND YOU - A COMPREHENSIVE GUIDE TO ORGANIZING A PROFITABLE HOME BASED CHILD CARE BUSINESS</u>

ISBN #0-943135-01-X

Retail Price: $19.95
Discount Price: $15.45

Author: PATRICIA C. GALLAGHER
Reviewed: BOOKLIST, February 1, 1987

2. <u>SO YOU WANT TO OPEN A PROFITABLE DAY CARE CENTER - A BASIC "HOW TO DO IT" GUIDE</u>

ISBN #0-943135-05-2

Retail Price: $12.95
Discount Price: $10.21

Author: PATRICIA C. GALLAGHER
Reviewed: BOOKLIST, October 15, 1987

3. <u>ROBIN'S PLAY & LEARN BOOK - HOW TO ENTERTAIN CHILDREN AT HOME OR AT PRESCHOOL</u>

ISBN #0-943135-10-9

Retail Price: $9.95
Discount Price: $7.96

Author: PATRICIA C. GALLAGHER

<u>DISCOUNT TERMS</u>

* QUANTITY DISCOUNTS for orders of twelve or more copies.

* First time customers, payment before delivery.

* Additional Orders: Payment due within 30 days.

* 1 1/2% Service Charge will be added to all invoices past 30 days.

* Reorders may be placed by calling 215-364-1945. Please leave your message and we will return your call promptly.

* There is <u>no postage and handling</u> charged for quantity orders.

ABOUT THE AUTHOR

Patricia C. Gallagher shares the experience, knowledge and the insights which have been used by many successful day care owners and directors.

This comprehensive book contains materials that can be readily adapted for your use, sparing you the time expenditure and research costs that went into its development. With many years of experience in the field of early childhood education, the author is a nationally recognized teacher, author and child care consultant. She is Director of Gallagher, Jordan & Associates, Education and Child Care Management Consultants.

She currently conducts day care organization and administration seminars for administrators, teachers, corporate personnel and individuals who are interested in opening day care centers.

She is the author of numerous journal articles, pamphlets and publications. Her first book **"Child Care And You! A Comprehensive Guide To Organizing A Profitable Home-Based Child Care Business"** was recommended as a "natural acquisition for public libraries" by the American Library Association. ($19.95)

"Robins's Play and Learn Book" is a fun filled discovery and idea book designed for anyone who works with young children. It is a new kind of arts and crafts manual that utilizes simple materials found in most homes. The games, poems, party themes and no-bake recipes will be enjoyed by child and adult. ($9.95)

Gallagher holds a Masters in Business Administration with concentration in Management and Finance. Educational degrees include graduate credits in Day Care Administration and a Bachelor of Arts in Elementary Education.

Do you need a gift for someone special? Write "GIFTWRAP" on your order and a card with your name and best wishes along with our beautifully packaged gift will be sent to the designated address.

All books are available from the publisher, **MAIL ORDER ONLY:**

Gallagher, Jordan & Associates
Box 555
Worcester, PA 19490

TABLE OF CONTENTS

Introduction

When I opened my first day care center in the early 1970's, its success had to have been fueled by my enthusiasm alone! Although I had a B.A. in Education and several years of experience as an elementary school teacher, I did not have the faintest idea of how to run a business.

I remember that it all happened rather quickly. Fortunately, things fell into place very easily and we opened our attractive, cheerfully decorated child care center within 3 months. Insurance concerns and day care regulations were not difficult issues, because mothers were not as active in the workforce and day care was not the "hot topic" that it is today.

For me, I knew that 1) I loved children and teaching, 2) I had a high energy level, 3) I wanted to start my own business, and 4) I was ready for a change from teaching in the school district.

* How did I go about it?
* Did I make a fortune?
* Was it a rewarding experience or a disappointment?
* What advice would I give to others now that I am fifteen years "older and wiser?"

In addition to actual day care center operations, I have added experience and education to my resume. Graduate work in early childhood had enhanced my knowledge of child development, and an M.B.A. in Finance aided in my understanding of management, accounting and the importance of the "bottom line" financially. During the past three years, I have acted as a consultant for employee sponsored child care and have lectured extensively on day care related topics. These experiences have led to many invitations to be a guest on national television and radio talk shows in my capacity as an advocate for quality child care.

Hopefully, in the pages that follow, you will learn by my mistakes. Yes, I earned a profit and found being a business owner to be a lot of fun but I also learned the importance of many other factors that contribute to the success or failure of a business.

This handbook attempts to provide practical, easy to read information that will help others who are considering the day care business. It is quite an involved process but certainly not impossible to complete if you are aware of the possible stumbling blocks. It is my desire to share my experience and research on a variety of topics including licensing, legal issues, special services, recordkeeping, health and safety, insurance, landlord and tenant relationships, obtaining city occupancy permits, advertising and promotion, etc. Factors contributing to the success of other programs have been shared throughout this publication. Related materials and resources are included so that by simply reading this book, you will be able to access additional free information. As a matter of fact, I advise you to sit down today and write out postcards to some of the selected resources on my list. Within a few weeks, your mailbox will be filled with excellent books, publications and pamphlets that will be sent to you at no charge.

1

My ideas are not complicated so I believe that by reviewing this book, you will be aware of the essential points of "How To Successfully Organize A Day Care Program."

So....do you still want to own a day care center?

Now, you are ready to begin your "Basic - How to do it Guide."

"AN INSIDER'S VIEW FOR SUCCESS"

When I opened my first center, I was not married and had no children of my own. As a provider of child care, I could offer care in a "limited way." I had no way of really understanding the working mother's feelings of guilt, heartbreak upon hearing her child cry, feelings of sadness as she pulled away from our driveway, or annoyance when her child's clothing got mixed up or lost. Now, as a mother who has been a consumer of day care, I view things quite differently. When I returned to work for a major corporation (as a marketing representative), I left my 3 month old daughter in a day care arrangement. It was that experience that really taught me the realities and dilemmas of the working parent. Now, I truly understand day care from both perspectives. Parents are really interested in finding the perfect center. There is nothing more precious to you than your child. It is imperative to find caring people who will really love your child. I know that in a commercial business, where a profit has to be made, it is easy to lose sight of the importance of nurturing and showing affection to each child frequently during the day but this is what will make your program a "winner." This is what parents want and what the children desperately need.

In your initial discussion with the parents, try your best to understand the day care parent's dilemma. Try to feel their "worry" with them and assure them that their child will be special to you, too! Answer their questions about homesickness, crying and clinging and explain the importance of a daily routine. Little children that are rushed by their parents to "Hurry up and eat," "Quick, put your coat on," "C'mon, get in your carseat" are the product of an unpleasant morning routine. This will affect their adjustment to the day care experience. Of course, the evening pickup should be at a slower pace, even though it's tempting to rush your child to "Hurry, we have to go home."

Since most people who are considering the organization of a day care facility have a teaching, nursing or social service background, I have not concentrated on curriculum planning. You probably have shelves of textbooks that can help you in that area. Also, new teacher aid products and learning materials are introduced each year so you will want to keep abreast of the "state of the art" innovations. What I have attempted to help you with are the "How To's" of maintaining good relationships with the parents, providing quality care for the children, promoting a favorable image, the importance of quality staff, maintaining a balanced budget and not overspending, and offering reminders about strict compliance with the intricacies of all state and local regulations.

Your own experiences and special talents, combined with the practical suggestions offered in this book are what it takes to get "off to a good start."

Best of luck in this extremely rewarding and challenging venture!

PART ONE: <u>AGENCIES TO CONTACT</u>

Where Do I Begin?

Opening a day care center in an outside facility requires extensive planning and attention to detail. Once opened, it requires not only a good educational background but also a strong business and management acumen. Most businesses fail because of poor recordkeeping and management practices.

Contact the State Licensing Bureau (see appendix).Regulations vary from state to state and from community to community. Obtain a copy of the regulations and work hand in hand with your licensing representative. Do not buy or lease a facility until you are sure that you can obtain a certificate of compliance from every regulatory entity. For example, in addition to state regulations, you will also need the local zoning approval, fire and safety approval, building code approval, etc. Unless you have a signed operating certificate from each agency, you probably will not be permitted to operate or could be closed down after opening for failure to obtain proper permission.

The Licensing Bureau will provide a booklet which will explain general requirements about: standards for staffing, ratios, staff responsibilities, staff qualifications, and building physical site considerations, equipment, program for children, staff and child health appraisal, food and nutrition, transportation, procedures for application & admission of children, child recordkeeping, employee recordkeeping, special program requirements and special exceptions to regulations. (Read and reread!)

The Zoning Bureau for your town or city will explain the local zoning ordinances that determine what types of businesses may operate in a particular area. You may find out who governs this by calling the police, mayor's office, city council or superintendent's office. Be sure to inquire what taxes must be paid on a particular location. You may be in for quite a surprise because of the exorbitant taxes which may make a particular location unfeasible. Before making any final decisions about purchasing or leasing a building, be sure that, in writing, the zoning official has stated that the building is cited as a day care center location. If it is not, a public hearing may be needed to get a special permit or variance. If you will have to renovate, add an addition or make any changes to the existing site, be sure that the zoning board has approved them in writing. Your lawyer should be involved with the zoning issue and should write a clause into any lease or purchase contract that will protect you should your plans fall through and you are not able to proceed with the day care center location. Just because it is zoned for day care does not mean that it will meet all of the requirements for final day care approval. The zoning approval is just one piece of the puzzle. Be sure to send for the publication, Legal Handbook For Day Care Centers. It covers in detail, topics such as what zoning is, state zoning enabling laws, zoning classifications, the typical ordinance, zoning treatment of day care, zoning flexibility, obtaining zoning

5

flexibility for day care, improving the zoning status of day care, etc. In 1987, the book was available by calling, 1-202-755-7944. It was printed by the U.S. Department of Health and Human Services, Office of Human Development Services, Administration of Children, Youth and Families, Office of Developmental Services, Washington, D.C., 20201. The publication number is DHHS (OHDS) 83-30335. If they say that it is no longer in print, ask where you can obtain a copy. This is a _free_ document that is a comprehensive resource on the legal aspects of establishing and operating a child care center. The authors are Lawrence Kotin, Robert Crabtree, and William F. Aikman, (1981).

You may also call NAEYC (National Association For The Education Of Young Children), 1-800-424-2460. The booklet will be available from them in the fall of 1987.

Building Code Inspections (may be called Department of Building Safety) are required before approval for a center is permitted. It is imperative that the facility is deemed safe for children. The inspectors will probably verify the condition of building construction, radiators, heating, electrical and plumbing systems, level of asbestos and lead paint, emergency exits, screens on windows, emergency lighting, etc. Even if you believe it is feasible to modify or fix the above areas, is it cost advantageous to do so? Also ask about the number of blueprints required to file, applications fees, etc.

Fire Safety Approval must be obtained. The local department will probably survey the building and will guide you as to the requirements for alarms, fire extinguishers (They must be recharged periodically), fire drill plans, numbers and types of fire doors required, type of roof, and periodic inspections. You will probably have to keep a fire drill log that is dated as you practice with the children. You should also ask their advice for emergency procedures in the event of tornados, gas leaks, blackouts, and chemical spills, which could also occur unexpectedly. (Do you have easy access for emergency vehicles?)

Licensing and Inspections may be another regulatory agency that will inspect for condition of electricity, plumbing, general building construction, number of exits, health and safety, etc. Ask your state licensing representative to provide you with a list of all agencies that you should contact for approval.

Sanitation and Board of Health Bureau's approval may be required if you are planning to serve food. All food service personnel should possess a Health Card or Statement of Health from the local Health Department or physician. Some states do not send inspectors to check facilities for compliance with local state standards. In such a situation, designated program personnel-with knowledge of applicable sanitation laws and regulations should check annually for compliance with these regulations and be responsible for the correction of existing violations. Written evidence of this must be available. Self-inspection reports should be completed to assure maintenance of standards. The following areas should be addressed: cleanliness and safety of food before, during and after preparation including maintenance of correct temperature; cleanliness and maintenance of food preparation, service, storage

6

and delivery areas and equipment; insect and rodent control; garbage disposal methods; dishwashing procedures and equipment; food handling practices; health of food service personnel; water supply. Local or state sanitarians in health agencies can be most helpful in providing ideas on ways to meet sanitation standards. Contact Child Nutrition Division, Food and Nutrition Service, USDA, 3101 Park Center Drive, Alexandria, VA 22302 for materials and information on Food Programs, and for suggested source of menus and recipes. Tested recipes are recommended to insure uniform quality, prevent waste and serve as a guide to purchasing. Other needed records include food and equipment inventories, personnel evaluation and training records.

The Federal Food Program is called the Child Care Food Program (CCFP) and it provides food money for some centers. This agency will be particularly interested in the cleanliness of the bathroom and kitchen facilities. You may also be required to hire a dietician. The dietician should be knowledgeable about appropriate portions for children's servings and balanced meal planning. You will probably be instructed to post the weekly meal plans for the parents to review. Due to cultural and religious variables, you may be asked to provide special dietary considerations for some children. The Board of Health will also scrutinize your storage areas, food preparation methods, waste disposal, and means of ventilation. If the cost of renovating a kitchen to serve meals is prohibitive, each child could bring a lunch.

PART TWO: <u>PROFESSIONALS TO CONTACT</u>

A Certified Public Accountant is absolutely necessary. Choose one that is recommended to you by another successful day care center. You will depend on this professional help for determining how your business will be set up. If you are not run by a government agency, an organizational structure must be determined (sole proprietorship, corporation, etc.) Your tax status will be determined by the type of organizational structure selected. A sharp accountant will show you a method of systematic record-keeping that will enable you to have a firm handle on your cash flow situation. (How much money came in and how much money was spent). Complex issues such as the paperwork required for tax purposes are best addressed by someone with the expertise in tax laws, deductions permitted, and sound accounting principles. All of the paperwork required by the IRS such as income tax returns, reports, forms, and notices can be confusing. Profit-making centers and non-profit centers will be treated differently by the IRS. The free Legal Handbook mentioned earlier also discusses these problems in detail.

Ask your accountant how he/she will handle the "Periodic Tax Returns" which employers are required to file quarterly to the Federal Government. The "Annual Tax Return" is required whether you are profit or non-profit and whether you made money or lost money on your business. (Due April 15th of each year). Be sure to clarify what functions will be performed and agree on a reasonable fee ahead of time. Other examples of IRS requirements are:

1. Withholding Exemption Certificate: You probably remember the forms that you have filled out when you started a new job. This certificate determines how much tax is withheld for federal, state and city income taxes. Forms are obtained from the IRS office and are needed for each of your employees.

2. Not for Profit Centers: These will most likely be required to file detailed financial reports. If you are operating under this status, be sure to understand the procedures so that you do not incur a penalty or loss of license.

Your accountant will advise you to save receipts for everything that you purchase. Tax laws change annually but keep in mind that allowable deductions may include all monies spent in transportation, mileage, equipment, food, gifts, supplies, professional journals and conferences, parties, etc.

A lawyer who has good, honest, and previous proven experience with day care issues is vital to the success of your center. (The lawyer who handled a friend's divorce may not have expertise in this field!) In addition to helping you determine the organizational form such as sole proprietorship, partnership, corporation, profit or not for profit, this expert can explain all of the intricacies about liability. There are issues such as financial liability and personal liability. We all know that people sue readily in this day and age so you want to understand liability. Your lawyer can also advise you about hiring practices. Remember that there are certain types of questions that you are not permitted by law to ask prospective employees. There are legal limits. It may be a sticky issue to question candidates for employment by asking them about height, weight,

sexual preferences, age, religion, race, etc. So that you are not faced with a Discrimination Lawsuit, seek the advice of your lawyer as it relates to Hiring/Personnel Practices. Your lawyer can advise you of current laws related to personnel.

Your lawyer or accountant can help you with business requirements such as obtaining:

1. Employer Identification Number: This is required if you hire salaried employees. A form is available from the IRS which is not complicated. (no fee)

2. State Unemployment Insurance (Department of Employment Security or Department of Unemployment Compensation): Most states require that you fill out forms that pose questions about your employees, tax status, type of business, etc. You must pay money into a fund that will be used as unemployment compensation. This is used if your employees go out on unemployment benefits. This procedure is handled differently for profit and non-profit.

3. Social Security : As an employer, you will have to pay FICA tax (Federal Insurance Contribution Act). This is a tax which is deducted from an employee's paycheck in a percentage amount but which also must be matched by you, the employer. (Non-profit centers are handled differently).

An Insurance Broker that is experienced with day care is critically needed. So many accidents are possible - you need this protection for yourself, your staff, volunteers, visitors, etc. There are many types of insurance coverage. Have a clear understanding of the following types of insurance: liability, health and medical, automobile, transportation, fire, theft, workmen's compensation, Fidelity Bonds (available to protect against financial wrongdoing by day care center employees), business interruption insurance, and life insurance. Insurance is a complex subject and can be quite costly. I would advise you to talk to other center owners. You should also call the National Association for the Education Of Young Children in Washington, D.C., (1-800-424-2460). As a member of their association, you may be able to obtain coverage through a large insurance company that is sponsoring a special program. The key is to shop around, not necessarily for the best price but for sufficient coverage at a reasonable premium. Of course, keep your center free of safety hazards but also maintain adequate coverage at all times.

What Types Of Incidents/Accidents Can Happen?

In recent conversations with day care owners, the following incidents occurred:
*   A baby bottle warmer with scalding hot water fell on a child
*   Several fingers were pinched in a swing set
*   A hand was crushed in a door which slammed shut
*   A child walked behind transportation van and was hit
*   A six month old baby died of sudden infant death syndrome
*   The teacher left one preschooler at the zoo (negligence law suit!)

10

* A toy shelf not bolted to the wall fell on a child and she suffered severe head injuries
* A child drowned in a swimming pool
* A toy box lid slammed shut and the child's neck was broken
* A driver left a group of children in a van while she went into a bank (very poor judgment!). Anyone engaged with driving children must have a proper license and adequate insurance coverage
* A child choked on a hot dog
* A child fell down while running with a pencil and punctured his cheek when he fell
* A door leading to the street was left unlocked and a child left the facility without anyone's knowledge
* Inadequate refrigeration of food led to spoilage which in turn sickened an entire center of 50 children
* Mother and child fell on slippery sidewalk outside of the center

None of the above information can be taken too lightly. I would advise you to work very closely with your state licensing representative so that you are sure that all bases are covered. Again, I caution you not to sign anything unless your lawyer has written in a contingency stating that all contracts, deals and agreements are null and void if all appropriate permits are not obtainable. In many cases, you could obtain waivers to certain regulations if you agree to complex and expensive changes but remember a day care center is not the easiest way to make you a millionaire so be careful about how you spend your money. Each of these departments and consulting experts will probably charge you reviewing and filing fees. Another important factor is that these licenses expire periodically, so be sure to have a renewal filing system so you can re-apply without incurring penalties and experiencing problems.

Cautions About Leasing Contracts

If you are new to this business, my advice would be to sign a one or two year lease with an option for renewal. Your business may be an overwhelming success or you may realize that there are some shortcomings that you did not anticipate. Your own personal situation could change too. You could marry, divorce, move to another state, etc., and a long term lease of 5 or 10 years would be a legal commitment that would oblige you to continue payments long after your center discontinued services.

Be sure to ask about rental increases. Are they scheduled or is the rate firm for the term of the lease? Who is responsible for lawn care, snow removal, repairs? Exactly what areas can be used? Can you use the building after hours?

My own "learning" experience was a "catch clause" written into the "fine print" of our agreement. The landlord not only received a monthly payment but also required a copy of our

financial statements to collect a percentage of our gross income. Of course, upon this discovery, we terminated our lease at the end of our legal obligations.

Be sure that an attorney assists you in all negotiations related to lease agreements. A clause of "pending approval" should be included in the negotiated document.

PART THREE: <u>ASSESSMENT OF DAY CARE NEEDS</u>

Is There A Need For Day Care In This Community And Where Should I Locate?

Before deciding on a perfect location, make sure that the area needs another center and that it is convenient for working parents (There are some areas that <u>need</u> day care but the parents will not be able to <u>afford</u> it). Ask yourself and others:

* Is the area in a high growth pattern? (Or are factories, plants and industries moving away?)
* Is there a large preschool population? (Drive through the neighborhood and observe).
* Are young professionals moving into the area? (Contact the Chamber of Commerce for business information).
* Is the proposed location close to corporate centers, shopping malls, factories, and office buildings?
* Is the site near major highways, residential areas and transportation?
* What kind of center is needed?
* What type of program is needed and what do you wish to offer?

In real estate promotion, the key phrase is "Location, Location, Location." Parents are looking for convenience - either close to home, close to work, or enroute to work. With all of the pressures of maintaining a home and work schedule, they usually do not want to go off the beaten track to drive to a day care center. Also, a brightly decorated, attractive looking facility, playground or sign may be one of your best and least expensive forms of advertising. If you are located where the traffic pattern is slight, you will be missing a good chance to "show off" your playground filled with happy children.

Although there may be several centers in one area, you may plan to cater to the needs of a new group. Think about your philosophy. Will you stress religion, academics (math and reading readiness) or play (socialization/group activities)? Be sure that you understand your target market and that they are willing and <u>able</u> to afford any special services that you may offer.

How Do I Find A Potential Site?

When starting to look for a potential site, it is wise to contact the city housing authority, the zoning board, and real estate first. Ask if they know of any buildings that <u>may</u> be suitable or may soon become available. Remember, they are not cognizant of all that is involved with day care regulations and local ordinances regarding day care so just consider these suggested locations as <u>possible leads</u>. One real estate person showed a home to a prospective day care center owner. She pointed out that it was perfect for a center because it was located on a main thoroughfare, had a great parking lot, an enclosed yard and lots of space for happy little children but, unfortunately, after the settlement papers were completed...the heartache began. Although it appeared to be a perfect location to the realtor and

the inexperienced day care operator, the site was not acceptable. Over $150,000 had been paid for a large home which was not able to be approved by the various regulatory agencies. The problem was an underground sewage system. The existing sewer facility did not have the capacity to handle the needs of 50 children and the staff. The cost to fight this issue and install a new sewer system was out of the question.

After selecting four possibilities, ask your licensing representative's opinion of each location (large house, vacated school building, factory, nursing home, hospital, church, synagogue, single story apartment complex or unit, community building, corporation, retail store, college campus, military facility, government office building, etc.) Ask your licensing representative about the pros and cons of each of the above locations. Be sure that the condition of the potential site is in sufficient state of repair in regard to sturdy construction of walls, floors, ceiling, etc.

When Is The Best Time to Open?

During the summer months, many people are on vacation and/or are reluctant to make day care changes. A "grand opening" in September, with registration accepted in the summer may be okay. Also, January is a good time - coinciding with the school semester. Summers are generally a slower period and enrollment is usually down. A Summer Camp for school age children may be organized to fill in for the absence of tuition payments from your regular students.

PART FOUR: <u>BUSINESS CONSIDERATIONS</u>

What Is The Profit Potential Of This Business?

There are many variables that affect profits. Some of the factors are: the number of children enrolled, the salaries of the staff, the ratio of staff to children required by your state regulations, how you control your expenses and the presence of a continued need for child care in your area.

There are innumerable factors that would have to be considered. I believe that you can make a comfortable living by owning a day care center but you will not become a millionaire overnight. Some experienced women have told me that their true net pay would be higher if they worked as a director at someone else's center because they would put in a 40 hour week and be paid for that amount of work. As an owner, you are involved each day. There is no doubt that you will be thinking about the business on the weekends. You may even have your family helping you clean, paint, and maintain the general appearance of your center by putting in time on Saturday and Sunday.

If you follow the advice in this guidebook and really do your homework about needs assessment, site location, and compliance with the rules of all regulatory entities, your risk factor should be low. Since day care is definitely an issue of the 80's, with anticipated growth in the 1990's, the emergence of quality day care centers should be welcomed.

Although it is more profitable to operate a large center because of the cost effectiveness of spreading the overhead expenses over a larger number of children, I would advise you to start out on a smaller scale. Unless you have a lot of experience in this area, you would be wise to start with about 25 children in a smaller location. If all goes well and you still enjoy the business with all of the inherent rewards and disappointments, you can always announce your "expansion plans." To jump right in and enroll 100 children or more is a grand responsibility.

What Do I Need To Start A Business?

Call the toll free hotline 1-800-368-5855, of the Small Business Administration. They can answer your questions about a wide range of subjects regarding how to get a loan, how to run a new business, etc. It is like having your own free business consultant!

1. Fictitious Name Approval: Selecting a catchy name for your center is important but you must be sure that no other business is operating using the same name. In some states, you register your name with the county and in others with the state. Request at least 3 copies of this approval. Be sure to ask if any other registration is required in your area. Your lawyer or licensing representative can help you file this simple form. A very small fee will probably be charged.

2. Bank Account: Begin a bank account and charge account in your business name right away so you can keep track of all of the

fees, charges, and expenses as they occur. Write checks or charge everything so that you have supporting documents at tax time. You will probably need a copy of your fictitious name approval at this point.

Where Can I Obtain Funding For My Day Care Center?

Bank Loans: Visit several banks. Be professional in all of your dealings. "Dress For Success" and have a typed Business Plan prepared. Your library or accountant can help you with books that will tell you how to prepare a plan which basically explains the amount of money that you need to borrow to start up your business and how you plan to pay it back. Your Accountant can help you estimate start up costs and operating expenses. In banking language, these are called "Start Up Budgets" and "Operating Budgets."

Grants: To learn how to apply for a grant, visit your library. In the reference section, you will find current directories of organizations, foundations and corporations that have funds to distribute. There is a special way to successfully approach obtaining a grant so take care in filling out requests precisely.

Private Investors: Ask local community organizations, businesses, the Chamber of Commerce, or PTA's if they would contribute money for a particular aspect of your business. Since you will be providing a service for their working community, they may be willing to help out with money for indoor and playground equipment, the infant room etc. Be sure to express your gratitude in writing via a letter to the editor of the local newspaper or a commemorative plaque posted conspicuously. This would be a good "news item" for the papers too!

Corporations or Nursing Homes: If you are experienced in day care administration or are well connected in business, you might approach corporations about on-site child care. Individuals who have sucessfully organized centers for employees stress that you should not approach the Personnel Department with your plan. Since corporate decisions are not made at the Personnel level, you should address your correspondence and follow up call to the President of the company. Day care centers in nursing homes are also beginning to grow in popularity. There is a "How To" book - Hand in Hand: A Guide to Intergenerational Programming which is available by sending $8.00 to: Hand in Hand, Route, 2, Box 297, Monticello, MN 55362.

Small Business Administration: (1-800-368-5855) This group can help you to locate sources of capital especially if you are a woman or a member of another minority group. Ask about SCORE which is a group of retired executives who are available to act as free consultants for any new business. They are an invaluable source of information and should be one of your priority contacts. Don't delay in contacting them.

State Regulatory Agency: Ask a knowledgeable state licensing representative if there are any grants, fellowships or monies set aside for centers that cater to a particular need. Perhaps you could qualify and save yourself the need for private investment funds.

What Costs And Expenses Do I Need To Consider?

This list is just a brief overview of some expenses that you will incur in the set-up and operation of a center. These costs will probably increase regularly so build that factor into your budget and tuition planning.

Advertising: postage, classfied ads, display ads, direct mail for publicity efforts, outdoor sign

Printing: flyers, brochures, enrollment forms, stationery, business cards, policy handbooks for employees and parents

Office Equipment: desk, chairs, lamps, filing cabinets, bookcase, typewriter, calculator, couch, copy machine, bulletin board

Office Supplies: stapler, purchase order forms, bookkeeping forms, filing folders, tabs, straight pins, thumbtacks, paperclips, fasteners, paper, tape, markers, calendar, glue, keys, ruler, appointment book, gummed labels

Security Deposits: rent, connection charges for utilities such as telephone, gas, electricity, water, refuse and leaf collection

Maintenance Supplies: brooms, buckets, mops, vacuum cleaner, waste baskets, paper products, cleaning supplies, bathroom supplies, rags, dishwasher detergent, laundry detergent, sponges, dustpan, cleanser

Professional Fees: lawyer, accountant, insurance premiums, licensing fees, other application fees

Renovation Expenses: carpenter, electrician, plumber. (Be extremely careful in site selection. What may appear to be a perfect location may be very costly if you have to replace wiring, add partitions, erect a fence, repair a leaking roof, etc.)

Maintenance Expenses: grounds maintenance, snow removal, carpet cleaning, window washing, exterminator service, repair of indoor and outdoor play equipment

Classroom Expenses: tables, chairs, cots, mats, TV, blackboard, record player

Miscellaneous: toys, games, puzzles, arts & crafts supplies (Buy in quantity), interest on borrowed money, cost of professional subscriptions, conferences, memberships, ongoing training for staff, fire extinguishers, first-aid kit, field trip costs.

What Are Other Major Expenditures?

Regulations vary from locale to locale but experienced

directors have told me of large expenditures for the installation of a commercial type kitchen with three sinks, an industrial type dishwashing machine and special laundry facilities, for washing sheets, diapers, etc. Separate bathrooms may be required (children/adult toilet areas, boy/girl areas or miniature sized sinks and toilets). What type of flooring is required? Do you need carpet, vinyl or both? Is an on-site playground required? Before you panic, check with your licensing representative for clarification.

What Should I Charge Per Week?

Tuition rates vary around the country. It is hard to believe but I have heard of fees as low as $25.00 and as high as $150.00 (1987 rates). Of course, if more than one child per family is enrolled, a discount is usually granted. Some schools charge a nominal pre-registration fee. This discourages parents from changing their plans at the last minute. If you call around to other centers, using an assumed name, you might ask for their rates. Often, the director will not quote this information over the phone and you will be invited to make an appointment. Perhaps a friend of yours with a preschooler could help you with this "research" by visiting centers, collecting brochures, asking questions about programs, etc. and then report back to you for "planning purposes." Your fees should be competitive and must be adequate to cover expenses for the type of day care to be offered, the hours of operation, the number of daily meals and snacks served, etc. Fees should be collected in a business like fashion and receipts should be given. Occasionally, fees might be waived or reduced according to hardship situations such as illness, or divorce. Experienced directors have stressed not to allow families to get behind in their payments - delinquent or unpaid balances may accumulate into uncollectable debts.

Several day care centers allow their parents to pay tuition using credit cards such as Mastercard or Visa. You should inquire about how to extend credit using this method of collecting fees. You could also offer a discount for those parents who pay you a month or two weeks in advance.

Remember that you will not reach full enrollment immediately. In interviewing one hundred directors for this guidebook, I was told that it took at least 6 to 9 months to reach 90% capacity. Also, because your operating expenses will increase annually, new tuition rates will be established each year. You will want to send a letter home to the parents well in advance telling of your intent to change the tuition. Be sure to explain that you are flexible in special cases so that the hardship is not too extreme for some families.

PART FIVE: <u>ADMINISTRATION</u>

What Types Of Forms Are Required?
(No liability is assumed with respect to the use of the information within)

Your state regulatory agency will provide you with the forms required. Examples of the types would be:

1. <u>Application For Day Care Service</u>: Date of application, name of child, address, birthdate, mother and father's home address, home telephone number, business telephone number, physician's name and telephone number, any special disability?, special medical, dietary or allergic conditions?, health insurance information and signature of parents, persons designated to pick up child, etc.

2. <u>Fee Agreement</u>: Fee charged and number of hours included, payment schedule, services included (child care, transportation, meals). Arrival and departure time.

3. <u>Child Health Appraisal</u>: Review of child's health history and special medical information to be filled out by physician. Includes immunization information and general developmental appraisal.

4. <u>Parental Consent</u>: This is usually the form taken with the child in case emergency medical care is needed. Includes name of day care facility, child's name, and written permission granted for emergency medical care. Also permission given for caregiver to administer prescription medicine (A list of all that can be administered and dosage). Also listed is a checklist for parental permission for field trips, swimming, transportation by facility, etc. Parent's signature and date.

5. <u>Accident Report Form</u>: Name of child, type of injury, date, time, details of accident, location, treatment provided, name of witness, signature. Consult your day care regulations for the situations which must be reported to the licensing agency.

6. <u>Staff Records</u>: Name, address, training experience, education, previous employment, health appraisal, written references, staff emergency information sheet.

7. <u>Fire Drill Record</u>: Record month, day and time of each fire drill.

8. <u>Master Medication Log</u>: Record date, name of child, medication and dosage administered, time, staff member who gave medicine.

9. <u>Field Trip Followup Form</u>: Would be a simple way to have teacher note the location of trip, points of interest visited, reaction of group, evaluation and comments, any special problems, accidents, signature and date, etc. As a director, you want to be apprised of everything that happens both within and outside of your facility.

10. <u>Progress Report for Parent Conferences</u>: The classroom teacher who is very familiar with the child should fill out the form which is designed to facilitate communication with the parents. A lot of thought should be given to each item before the parent/teacher conference. Usually included is a checklist which elicits a response as to how the child reacts to being without parents all day, child-group relationships, relationship with adults, ability to share, level of participation, adaptation to day care routine, activity preferences, any signs of emotional/physical discomforts, child's social behavior, napping and meal patterns, unusual behavior noted, observation of physical health etc. Be sure to allow time for parents to ask questions and make suggestions.

11. <u>Authorization to Release Information about Child</u>: Occasionally, you may see some children that you believe have special needs. You <u>may not</u> contact centers such as psychological and diagnostic services on behalf of the child without written permission from the parents. A form should be designed that would authorize you to furnish pertinent information concerning the child and the family. Failure to do so could result in legal responsibility.

12. <u>Parent Suggestions Form</u>: In order to improve services for the families, you may want to make a form available for comments. A suggestion box could be provided or the parents could discuss these issues at a Parents meeting. Also, ask the parents for ideas for a Parents Discussion group. Speakers from organizations would present topics of interest to working parents.

13. <u>Volunteer Forms</u>: Should be filled out as completely as an employment application. (including verified references, physical examination, criminal clearance, etc). In addition to the usual questions, ask about special interests or training in health, art, music, dance, athletics, etc. Specify the amount of time to be volunteered and inquire as to why they feel that they would make a good volunteer in a day care center. (A trial period should also apply to volunteers).

14. <u>Supply Requisition form</u>: As your housekeeping, arts & crafts, and snack supplies are consumed, you will want your staff to keep you informed so that you may reorder before the inventory has been depleted. The form should include: (1) Date, (2) Item Needed, (3) Amount Needed, (4) On Hand Amount, (5) Teacher's Name.

15. <u>Observation forms</u>: Day care workers who are involved with children for long periods of time are usually able to identify some problems which may need attention. You may design a form to note unusual activities such as:

temper tantrums	restlessness
hyperactivity	lethargic behavior
poor coordination	headaches, stomach aches
hearing or vision problems	rash, bruises, sores

frequent urination	restless during sleep
afraid of being alone	generally not satisfied
afraid of adults	sad disposition
afraid of strangers	moodiness

16. <u>Daily Infant Form</u>: Parents like to know the daily routine of their baby, so a form should provide information about: feeding schedule, quantity consumed, sleeping pattern, vomiting, fever, diaper rash, any reactions to food or milk, problems or worries, additional supplies needed, such as powder, baby food, bottles, ointment, etc.

Additional Recommended Forms

These forms are not required however I have found them to be useful.

1. <u>Checklist for Safety</u>: Make a list of all of the possible safety hazards and at least once a week, evaluate by checking your center against the safety list. (Are doors unobstructed? Is all equipment in good repair? Are bathroom and kitchen facilities sanitary?)

2. <u>Application for Professional Employment</u>: Preprinted forms can be purchased at a business supply store or you may design your own. Ask your lawyer if there are any questions that you may not ask on this form. There are usually lines included for name, address, telephone number, health data, emergency contact information, present and previous employment information history, education completed, additional training or relevant coursework, special qualifications, reference information etc.

3. <u>Authorization Form to Contact Previous Employer</u>: As a reference, this form is designed so that the prospective employee authorizes you to contact the past employers or references in order to pose questions about the suitability for employment.

4. <u>Staff Evaluation Form</u>: You will want to conduct performance evaluations with your staff on a regular basis. A form should be designed that rates a teacher or an aide on the following job performances: punctuality, reliability, good judgment, relationships with children, parents, and staff, attitude. Under their personal qualities: friendliness, warmth, sense of humor, understanding of children, tolerance, patience, flexibility, cooperation, professional attitude, etc. Of course, you are bound to think of many other traits to add to the list.

What Are Some Tips On Staff Selection?

How does an employer determine who to hire for a particular job? What interview techniques are most useful? How does an applicant assess her desire for and satisfaction with a particular kind of job? Day care center administrators may find the following suggestions helpful in interviewing applicants for staff positions.

In a job interview, the administrator should know the questions he/she wishes to ask and should encourage questions of the applicant. While it is hard to determine an applicant's ability to work with children solely from an interview, the administrator can attempt to judge the applicant's attitudes toward children, toward discipline and toward new ideas. A trial period from four to eight weeks is advisable for staff members, so both administrators and employees can test their abilities in working with children and other staff members. Procedures for terminating jobs without undue strain should be set.

Finally, administrators should arrange for potential staff members to talk with other people in their field, and to share ideas about the work involved at day care centers.

What About Administrative Procedures?

A director, the staff, and the parents share the responsibility for seeing that a day care center program runs smoothly and meets the needs of the children and their families. To facilitate this kind of administration, the following suggestions are presented.

1. Establish a grievance procedure, so every staff member and parent will know how and where to express complaints, and can voice opinions through established channels.

2. Have frequent informal sessions to discuss problems or special conditions long before a major crisis erupts.

3. Stress open acknowledgment of, and sensitive awareness to, possible difficulties when there are ethnic differences between staff and children.

4. Develop good communication between staff and parents. Parents should be included, whenever possible, in the decision-making processes.

5. Be responsive to each individual staff member as a human being, with a life both inside and outside the center.

6. Do not allow the center to be exclusively child-centered, although the primary staff function is care of children. Children need to experience the world of adults as it touches their lives, in order to learn their place in that world.

7. Assign parents working as staff members to a room or section other than that where their own children are placed. It is

difficult for both child and parent to develop new ways of relating to each other, and it is unfair to other children if one is singled out for special attention and care.

8. Tell staff members when they are succeeding and when they need to re-evaluate their behavior as staff members.

9. Consider the need for staff counseling at all levels. A counselor who helps with personal and professional problems is important in this kind of personally exhaustive work.

10. For a smoothly functioning staff, be willing to adapt to the needs of both adults and children. Many employees will be women with their own families. Often, complicated day care arrangements must be made to free them to work.

11. Remember that staff members grow and change. Continuing to treat someone as a trainee long after he/she is a fully-functioning member of the staff may lead to dissatisfaction and disappointment.

12. Turnover may be a major problem, and to minimize this, eliminate some of the most frequently disturbing situations leading to resignations, such as long hours, limited opportunities for advancement, lack of privacy, uneasy relations with other staff members, difficult children to care for without extra support, high demands on the stamina and physical energy of the staff, and low salaries.

13. Clarify work arrangements. Don't assume that a job description, once given, is completely absorbed and understood.

14. Provide opportunities for constant learning and outside stimulation. It is all too easy to become bored by working exclusively with infants and young children all day. To prevent this, staff members might occasionally exchange duties. Also, arrangements could be made for staff to attend special meetings and conferences, observe in other centers, and have discussions with other staff member about children and on-the-job- problems. Outside speakers can be invited to talk at staff meetings and abundant, interesting reading material can be made available.

What Is The Staff-Child Ratio?

To guarantee optimal development of infants and young children in group care, a low ratio of children to caregivers is preferable. High quality of a few will not make up for an insufficient number of caregivers. But neither will a large number of caregivers substitute for quality care. Caregivers who must supervise large number of children may neglect certain children and become exhausted. States differ in their licensing requirements regarding ratios. The average ratio recommended is one caregiver for each three children under one year of age, one for each four

to five children from one to two, and one staff member for each six children between two and three years old. Ideal ratios might come closer to one caregiver for each four children under two years of age, and one caregiver for every five children between two and three years of age.

What Are Some Characteristics Of Good Caregivers?

Obviously, no one person will have all the qualities described here. Initially, however, a caregiver should already have some of these characteristics; others may be acquired through training and experience. In general, the following qualities are important for a good caregiver:

1. She should be patient and warm toward children. This warmth is the basic ingredient in the caregiver-child relationship. Only with patience can the child be helped to develop, and the caregiver survive the strains of this type of work.

2. She should like children, be able to give of herself to them, and receive satisfaction from what they have to offer. She must be able to appreciate the baby as an individual, since this is vital to his growing self-acceptance. A caregiver also needs to have a sense of humor.

3. She should understand that children need more than simple physical care. She should have some knowledge of the practical care of children and be willing and able to learn from other people.

4. She must be able to adjust to various situations, understand feelings, and help children to handle fear, sadness and anger, as well as to experience love, joy and satisfaction.

5. She should be in good health. Since children possess abundant energy, the caregiver must herself be energetic and imaginative in order to teach and discipline them.

6. She must be aware of the importance of controlling undesirable behavior, but must not be excessively punitive or given to outbursts of anger.

7. She needs to show initiative and resourcefulness in working with children and be able to adapt the program to meet their individual needs and preferences.

8. She must be acquainted with, accept and appreciate the children's cultures, customs and languages if they are different from her own. Helping the child develop a sense of pride in his own uniqueness is vital.

9. She must respect the child and his parents, regardless of

their backgrounds or particular circumstance, thus helping the child learn to respect himself. Her own self-respect will aid her in imparting this quality to others.

10. She should be able to work with other adults and get along with the other staff members in order to provide a harmonious atmosphere at the center.

11. She should have a positive interest in learning, understand the importance and variety of learning needs in a young child, and be responsive to the child's attempt at learning in all spheres.

Should I Use Volunteers As Staff In The Day Care Center?

The use of volunteers in a day care center is a debatable topic. Their interest in children and their help can add to the program. However, volunteers should not work directly with children unless they show a great aptitude for this kind of work, and agree to accept supervision. A volunteer who appears on some days and not on others may destroy the continuity of care for children and the morale of other staff members. Therefore, volunteers should be required to commit themselves to a definite schedule of service, although their schedules may be more flexible than those of the regular staff. In this way, the volunteers become regular, contributing and necessary members of the day care staff.

(Reprinted with permission (1987), U.S. Department of HEW, Publication #OHDS-78-31056.)

PART SIX: ADVERTISING AND PROMOTION

How Can I Publicize My Business?

There are many ways to advertise. Advertising in the newspaper and phone book can be expensive. Some ideas that are less costly would be:

1. Obtain the names and addresses of the local newspapers. Send a "Press Release." Books in the library under "Public Relations" will tell you the precise format for writing a release that will have a good chance of appearing in the paper. A press release is just a short article about your business written in the third person. It must be written like a news story stating, "Who, What, Where, When, and Why." It cannot sound like you are asking for free advertising although that is precisely your intention. Review the style of most articles in your local paper that pertain to church bazaars, school events, town meetings, pet shows, etc. They are written by the organization and are a great way of obtaining free publicity. You must publicize your own business on a regular basis. At least four times a year, stage some newsworthy event and send out press releases.

2. Call the local "newsroom" of each paper and tell them that you are opening a new business in the area. They may want to do a "feature story" about you or some interesting aspect of the business. Try to think of an "angle" that makes your center sound special.

3. If you know of any free lance newspaper reporters, give them a call. They may want to write a story (complete with pictures) which they would sell to a newspaper. Be sure to make it sound like news not asking for free publicity.

4. Have a "grand opening party" to coincide with registration so that you may offer a tour of the facility so prospective parents can meet you and acquaint themselves with a few of your teachers. A cheerfully decorated center and a safe outdoor play area can help make "the sale." Be sure to be extremely organized, courteous and professional in the operation of your business. Hire a clown to give out lollipops and balloons, offer pony rides, or pay a musician to play children's songs on a piano or banjo. Don't forget to call the local TV news stations, newspaper, etc., to tell them about the event.

5. Occasionally, throughout the year, hold some social or special event. Be sure to call reporters and send press releases to provide information about your puppet performance, parade, baby contest, children's used clothing exchange, family movie night, magic show, Easter Egg Hunt, Breakfast With Santa, pony rides, ballet recital, child safety program, graduation ceremony, other holiday celebrations, penny auction, etc. Serve light refreshments. (This is good public relations).

6. Contact the personnel departments, school districts, real estate firms, civic organizations, etc, and tell them of your new

31

business. Send them a professional looking letter or flyer announcing your service (One page only). Since this is a reflection on you, be sure to have someone proofread it for spelling, grammar and general appearance. You only get one chance to make a good first impression. You will have to print brochures, flyers, and business cards. You may find a local independent printer who is less expensive than a stationery store or franchise printer. (Be sure to look at samples of the work before ordering).

7. Consider it "news" and call reporters if you decide to add any new services: sick child day care, full day kindergarten, senior citizen day care, drop-in babysitting, weekend and evening child care, holiday or summer care, handicapped care, twenty-four hour care, or if you decide to offer transportation service. Other centers have lessons in ballet, gymnastics, music, swimming--all for an additional fee.

8. If a parent has volunteered to demonstrate some special skill or talent at your center, let the media know about it. Small local newspapers are anxious to list these types of things in their calendar of events. How about a special one-hour seminar explaining the Child Care Tax Credit, if applicable?

9. One center prepared taped recordings that changed weekly on a separate phone number. The 3-minute message discussed a topic of interest to parents. Each week, the newspaper printed the topic, the phone number and the name of center (good free advertising and great public relations).

10. Design a colorful flyer. Make copies. Modify the sign to suit your program and your credentials. Make a pocket out of construction paper to hold your flyers. Decorate the construction paper with cut outs from magazines--pictures of mothers, children, etc. Post in supermarkets, community bulletin boards, libraries, churches, pediatrician's office, laundromats, and wherever parents congregate.

11. If your newspaper has inexpensive advertising rates, you may be successful by placing an ad in the classified or display ad section. People usually have to see something repeated about five times to be effective, so advertising in a newspaper can't just be done on a one time basis. Advertise continuously in one way or another. Be sure to have your center listed by any free referral services for child care.

12. Many day care centers have said that word of mouth has been their best form of advertisement--the percentage of new clients enrolled is greatest when satisfied parents spread the good word. Ask each parent how they heard of your center. After enrollment, send them a thank you note which explains your desire to make it a very pleasant experience for their family.

13. Hold a "Parents Night Out." This could be a time when you

offer discussion periods or lectures on career/day care related topics such as: child abuse, stress, child rearing issues, managing work and family, etc.

14. Place an ad in the Yellow Pages.

15. Make sure that your outside sign and facility is attractive, eye-catching and neat.

16. Tell everyone that you know about your business (friends, relatives, neighbors, acquaintances).

What Else Can I Do For Promotion?

In an Art Supply or Book store, you will find books called "Clip Art" or "Dover Art." These are books filled with logos (pictures) which are not usually covered by copyright legislation (so you are able to use these cute pictures on your stationery, brochures, business cards, etc.) The illustrations in this book are from "Clip Art" type books and each picture costs about twenty cents.

Contact local radio and talk shows and ask to be a guest. Believe it or not, the smaller ones in your area will probably schedule you immediately! You could offer to talk about any day care related topic such as "What Parents Should Look For In Quality Centers," "How Does Day Care Affect Children?" or any subject about early childhood development. Of course, this is great exposure for your center and a fun experience for you.

Finally, even the large television stations have "slow news" days. Our center was featured on all three of the major networks. There really was no special news about it initially, but roving reporters covered it at different times and we received excellent recommendations. One comical situation was right after we opened. The enrollment was about 10 children and two staff members. The center was beautifully decorated and equipped, however we were just starting out. A TV news reporter called and said that the mini-camera van was in the area covering another major event and they had noticed our "Grand Opening" sign. They were on their way to pay us a visit. Since I only had about a half hour before they would arrive, I quickly ran to the local Acme market and the library and told all mothers with small children that if they wanted their children on the evening news to quickly comb their hair, wash their faces and like the "Pied Piper", follow me. By the time the TV reporter arrived, we had a center filled with beautiful children playfully using all of the equipment and having a wonderful time. A staged performance? Yes! Successful exposure, without a doubt!

Another promotional attempt was when we rented two "attention getting" costumes. An 8 foot Big Bird and a 7 foot Dalmation were hard to ignore. It's hard to believe that we did this, but it did have the desired effect. My associate and I donned the extremely heavy and hot costumes and stood on a major highway causing everyone to look twice. Armed with hundreds of flyers and

balloons with our center's name, we passed out our promotional pieces. We even walked around several industrial complexes. Of course, we prayed that no one would even think it was us. Our hope was that people would think that we had hired high school freshmen for this "job." The results were remarkable! Several newspaper photographers thought it was a little odd so they snapped pictures which appeared in the evening newspaper along with our day care center's name. Just another means of publicity and exposure but it was worth the $80.00 costume rental fee.

When people see "Sitting Service," they may approach you with another caregiving need other than for children. One very nice man stopped in and asked if we might be able to help him with "birdsitting" for his two zebra finches. He had to go to California for two weeks and had no one to feed them. He thought, and we foolishly agreed that the birds in their decorative cages would be interesting for the children. He came in the next week and attached hooks for the cages and proudly told us of all of the precious moments and joys of raising his two <u>rare</u> babies. You guessed it! Both of them died during his absence. We fed them, talked to them, sang with them and provided excellent "aviary" care. Apparently they did not like the air conditioning. After worrying needlessly while we waited for the "proud papa" to return, we were surprised to find out he wasn't at all upset. Moral of Story: **Make Child Care your specialty!** "No Bird Watching" should be a part of you policy.

PART SEVEN: <u>ADVICE FROM THE EXPERTS</u>

Timely Tips From "Experienced Directors"

During research for this chapter, we interviewed many day care directors and asked for their input. Their advice is as follows:

1. Be clear about the level of education required to be a director, teacher, or owner of a center. (Are you sure that you qualify?) I know of two sisters whose father bought them a house so they could open a center. They did not have the background and the investment was a total loss.

2. Beware of long term leases or leases that are not advantageous to you. Landlord and tenant must agree in writing about the proposed use of the facility: (1) Are you permitted to add on?, (2) Are there any limitations to the site's use?, (3) How will you mediate disputes?, (4) Will you be allowed to use outdoor space for playground?, (5) Can you erect a fence?, (6) Can you use space after normal day care hours for meetings?, (7) Agree on rental fee and time availability of building, (8) Be sure that all plumbing and sewer systems are operable. (9) Decide who will be responsible for repairs, maintenance, snow removal, lawn care, etc.

3. Can a basement level be used for a center, or second or third floor? What special considerations are required?

4. Investigate which state agencies or community resource groups can provide free staff training on safety, nutrition, preschool programs, first-aid, etc.

5. Is academic school registrations required in your state? If so, what additional requirements must be met?

6. Must hot meals be served? What special food/kitchen equipment is required? Can kitchen help be a teacher or must you hire a cook and nutritionist to prepare food?

7. Be clear about amount of playground space and indoor space required for each child. You may not have to have your own playground if there is a playground located in close proximity. Check the regulations in your state.

8. Make sure zoning rulings will allow you to place a sign in front of your facility (What size and type is permitted). Do they have any restrictions about traffic patterns or parking arrangements?

9. Have a small "sick room" with a comfortable bed for a child who is waiting for his parents to pick him up. Children should be inspected each morning as a health check. If you determine he is sick, he should not be admitted.

10. Even if your enrollment is at capacity or if you are

unable to help a parent because of a specific situation, be extremely helpful. This parent will spread the word about how cordial you were. This is good for future business and a credit to your reputation.

11. Before signing a lease or purchase agreement, what would be a realistic determination for costs of remodeling, renovating, construction, alterations, repairing, upkeep for kitchen, bathroom, playroom parking lot, laundry room? Would you have to add storage closets, shelves, carpeting, linoleum, additional lighting, improved ventilation, fire escapes, new asphalt for lot, new heater, electrical wiring or new roof?

12. Be sure that staff members know their roles, school philosophy, and responsibilities. (Remember that your staff can make or break the reputation and ultimate success of your business). Be clear about the staff following your safety standards and approved methods of discipline.

13. Keep aware of morale and motivation problems. Be good to your staff. Help them to keep up their enthusiasm and avoid burnout. Low salaries and the absence of benefits are the main reasons for quick turnover of day care employees.

14. Be sure to have a list of competent and approved substitutes. Make certain that they meet minimum age requirements and that they have a valid criminal/fingerprint clearance as determined by your state's regulations.

15. Develop an Employee Handbook which details hiring policies, salary range, benefits, absence policies, holidays, vacation, expectations in working with children and parents, classroom and playground rules, etc. Review this with each prospective employee and discuss frequently at staff meetings so that you are aware of any "gripes." You want to keep your employees satisfied, so it's best to listen to their suggestions.

16. Develop a Parent Handbook so that sensitive communication with parents is more easily facilitated. It should include: sick policy, fee payment schedule, payment of late fees, arrival & dismissal procedures, parent contract, field trip explanation, extra clothes needed. One unhappy parent can cause a great deal of damage to your reputation.

17. "Perception" is important. How parents perceive you, your staff, your facility, your treatment and attitude towards children are critical. Do everything that you can to make sure that your center and staff are impressive. Handle everyone like glass!

18. Create a warm welcome for the parent and the child when they arrive. If possible, the owner should be there throughout the entire day. Parents like to see that continuity.

19. Double the time that you think will be required to open a day care center. Some of the delays in opening will be beyond your control since there may be confusion among the many regulatory agencies. You should plan to be in the center at least a month before opening to make sure that everything is in place and that all necessary documents have been obtained.

20. Contact Vocational Technical Schools and Senior Centers to help you build special projects. Of course, make sure that the equipment is built to your exact safety standards because you are ultimately liable for everything that happens in your center.

21. Supplies are expensive. Don't hesitate to send memos home occasionally asking parents to save styrofoam meat trays, computer paper or other things that their place of employment may be throwing away. (Be sure to read the page "What Parents Can Save", which is included in this book.)

22. Take a course at a local adult evening school on Small Business Management, so that you will be familiar with Tax Liability, Recordkeeping, Legal Aspects, Incorporation, etc. In addition to knowledge about day care, to be successful, you must also have sound business, financial and management skills.

23. Visit other day care centers. Of course, due to the threat of competition, many local directors will not be too anxious to help you out so visit centers in other nearby cities. Observe their programs. If possible, try to obtain a copy of their "Parent Handbook" as a guide for planning your own.

24. Call 1-800-424-2460 (NAEYC) and ask for the telephone number of the local NAEYC Chapter. Attend their meetings as a means of networking. Experienced day care directors and teachers will share their expertise with you if you are a member of this excellent association.

25. Contact the Early Childhood Department of local colleges for substitutes, teachers or just advice on quality early childhood programs. Some traits of competent staff workers are friendliness, a high energy level, good judgment, the ability to instill confidence with the parents, be well adjusted, and love children. Check all references thoroughly.

26. Have a newsletter or bulletin board available for parents to list carpool arrangements, exchange services and ideas, sell used items, etc. Some system for sharing daily happenings with the parents should be implemented. How about a small library for parents to share books about raising children? Some centers send a calender of events home each month to keep parents apprised of special events such as field trips, parents night, etc.

27. Don't forget to consider replacement costs and utility rate increases when planning your budget. Equipment wears out, supplies are consumed and phone, electric and water costs do not

remain constant.

28. Transportation costs include vehicles, insurance premiums, inspections, maintenance, oil, gas, etc. Be sure all of this is considered when setting your fees.

29. Occasionally, you will have uncollectable fees (People withdraw children without notice or payment). It is recommended to have parents pay a week in advance and notify you two weeks in advance of plans for withdrawal.

30. You may want to recruit volunteers from community colleges, local universities, and nursing schools (Pediatric nursing students may have to study the "Well Child"). It is advisable to have a definite plan of activities for them to follow. Be sure that volunteers meet the qualifications of your state licensing bureau and are covered by the fine print of your insurance policy. Since this practice teaching may be considered as their internship or student teaching, be sure to give them responsible tasks and monitor their progress so you can report back to their instructors.

31. Perhaps parents can trade reduced fees for their help with repairs, sewing, landscaping, reading stories, typing, help with fundraising activities, offering parent workshops in a field that would interest other parents, etc.

32. Explain to the parents the importance of not rushing the children in the morning at drop-off or in the evening at pick up time.

33. Children can feel depressed when home life is in turmoil. (divorce, death, sickness, family fighting, parent away on business trip). Staff must be trained to be aware of changes in behavior and temperment. Ask the parents to let you know about anything that may make the child anxious so that your staff can offer extra understanding.

34. Be sure to do everything "First Class." First impressions are lasting! Your facility should be clean and uncluttered. Your staff should be warm and loving. Your brochures and signs should all be professionally and attractively printed.

35. Have a "First Anniversary" party of your day care center to show off the facility, creative art projects, staff, etc.

36. Fundraisers could be the sale of T-shirts, candy, baked goods, etc. Consider having a Flea Market or Craft Fair and offering exhibit tables for rent.

37. Even if you plan to be affiliated with a church, contact the licensing bureau in your state to clarify the requirements as they relate to church status.

38. A successful day care business usually depends on an owner/operated facility. Turning the reins of management over to a manager is risky. No one cares about the success as much as you do. (In my experience I have seen several cases where a trusted employee was tempted by the collection of cash and loose recordkeeping. The absentee owners lost a substantial amount of money before the loopholes were discovered). As a director, you should be involved with the teachers and children. "Pop in" regularly to each classroom and observe. Unless you keep a watchful eye on every aspect of the care offered in your center, you might not be aware of what is <u>really</u> going on.

39. Keep expenses under control! It is tempting to buy fancy equipment but remember that most businesses fail due to excessive spending and poor recordkeeping.

40. Provide money for staff training at workshops, conferences and for renting movies on child development and day care issues. Let your staff know that you are interested in furthering their professional development.

41. Establish a working relationship with a local pediatrician so that he/she can be "on call."

42. Network with local day care associations so you are plugged into problems, legislative issues and new resources.

43. Don't underestimate problems which are associated with asbestos in a building, lead paint, fire alarms, noise levels which may not be acceptable to neighbors, and parking problems.

44. Many people are just "shopping" by calling every center in the phone book. Rather than give too much information over the phone, take their name and phone number and set up a time for them to visit your center. After greeting the parent and child warmly, take them on a tour and follow up with an informative package that includes brochure, fee schedule, general policies, and procedures, etc. Be sure to give the parent plenty of time to ask questions.

45. Don't overlook the possibility of using your center during "off hours" for evening and weekend babysitting.

46. Don't overlook buying used equipment. Check the Sunday newspaper for auctions of office furniture, paper products, general supplies. Many businesses fold and are anxious to recoup some of their money by selling their assets.

47. Your staff should all be trained in emergency First Aid procedures. Ongoing staff training in all areas contributes to the success and professionalism of your center.

48. Have a trial period for new staff members.

49. Learn of all of the resources in your state that may apply to children who have special needs.

50. As the owner, your enthusiasm will be contagious. Don't remain aloof from staff and children. I can't emphasize enough how important it is for you to be involved. (Don't hide in your office with administrative details.)

51. You can recruit handymen to help with basic repairs, paint up, and fix up. Contact college students, retired people or the city youth program. Place ads in local newspapers. Check references and agree on fees charged for service. Workmen should only be present on weekends or after hours. No work should be done while the children are in the building. You could also ask parents if they are able to recommend competent and dependable workers.

52. A parent newsletter could be used to offer helpful hints on child care and early childhood development, to inform parents of special art projects, parties, words to songs, and learning activities so they can reinforce what is being introduced at the center. Also use the newsletter as a means to inform parents of how they can become more involved with the program.

53. Although infant day care is in demand, state regulations require a high adult to infant staff ratio. Keep this in mind when planning staff needs and tuition charged for infant day care.

54. Imagine yourself being a child in a day care center! Remind your staff to do the same. From this vantage point you will be able to give the children your best!!

55. Don't be discouraged. It takes some time to reach full enrollment. (Keep repeating the ideas in the Publicity section of this book).

How Will Parents Evaluate Your Center?

Since day care is a very "hot topic," most women's magazines have written articles, with a checklist for "comparison shopping" for day care service. The parents will probably evaluate your center and your ability to provide care by using questions such as those listed below.

1. Is the center license current? Where is it posted?

2. What would you do if my child became ill? Is there an isolation area? Would you notify me right away? How is an emergency procedure handled?

3. Can parents visit child during lunch hour? Are parental visits encouraged? Can parents drop-in unexpectedly?

41

4. Would my child feel comfortable here? Is the center child oriented? Are the children touched patiently, lovingly, gently?

5. Do the building and playground appear safe for children? Is the center adequately staffed? Do you believe the number of staff can effectively supervise the children?

6. Are the rooms bright, attractive, uncluttered and well organized?

7. What is the weekly menu? What types of snacks and drinks are provided? Are meal plans posted? Are meals nutritious?

8. Is the outdoor play equipment clean and safe?

9. Are inside toys age-appropriate, and in good repair?

10. Do you like the caregivers? Are they warm, open, sensitive, flexible and loving? Do they communicate with children in their "own language?" Can you establish a friendly relationship with the staff?

11. What is the philosophy of the center? Does the staff understand what curriculum they employ? Are there interesting bulletin boards, art learning projects on display?

12. Would you feel at ease discussing your concerns? Would the staff be willing to accept constructive evaluation from parents? Will the center honor your individual requests?

13. What are the discipline procedures? What are napping procedures? Do the children appear well rested?

14. What are diaper changing procedures? Is the diaper area disinfected after each child? Are you satisfied with the toilet facilities? Is the center sanitary? Do the children look clean and healthy?

15. Is there a shady area to play so children are protected from intense rays of the sun? (Sliding boards and other metal equipment may be too hot to use in the summer.)

16. Are there learning activities for each age group? Do they understand the importance of providing a wide variety of experiences for young children?

17. How does the center celebrate holidays, birthdays, etc? Is the staff understanding of cultural and ethnic differences?

18. What types of academic training do the teachers have?

19. Are seat belts/car seats provided for field trips?

20. Do the children look happy? Is there a healthy noise level

of the center? Can the staff give you references from other parents who use the center?

21. Do you understand the center's policies on vacation days, withdrawal procedures, payment of fees, late charges? Are the fees comparable with other centers in the area?

22. Will the schedule meet the needs of your child?

23. How will the staff communicate with you about your child's day? Will they have time to chat each day? An evening phone call? Progress reports? Will a written memo be provided? Are home visits scheduled?

24. Will there be "Open Houses" and conferences scheduled regularly?

25. Can parents volunteer to go on field trips or help out with special events?

26. Are the exits from the classroom and building unobstructed for easy escape in an emergency?

PART EIGHT: EDUCATIONAL CURRICULUM GUIDANCE

Educational Curriculum Guidance

The Education Plan should indicate:

1. How the Education Program will provide children with a learning environment and varied experiences appropriate to their age and stage of development which will help them develop: socially, intellectually, physically, emotionally.

2. How the Education Program will integrate the educational aspects of the various components in the daily program of activities.

3. How the Education Program will involve parents in educational activities to enhance their role as the principal influence on the child's education and development.

4. How the Education Program will assist parents to increase knowledge, understanding skills, and experience in child growth and development.

5. How the Education Program will identify and reinforce experiences which occur in the home that parents can utilize as educational activities for their children. The plan should be accompanied by brief descriptive information regarding: geographical setting, physical setting (available facilities), populations to be served (ethnicity, race, language, age, prevalance of handicapping conditions, health factors, family situations), education staff (staffing patterns, experience, training), volunteers, community resources, program philosophy/ curriculum approach, assessment procedures (individual child, total program).

How To Enhance Children's Understanding Of Selves

The following suggestions may be useful beginning steps: encourage awareness of self through the use of full-length mirrors, photos and drawings of child and family, tape recordings of voices, etc.

How To Give Children Opportunities For Success

Here are some examples:

1. Make sure that activities are suited to the developmental level of each child.

2. Allow the child to do as much for himself as he can.

3. Help the child learn "self-help" skills (pouring milk, putting on coat).

4. Recognize and praise honest effort and not just results.

5. Support efforts and intervene when helpful to the child.

6. Help the child accept failure without defect ("I will help you try again.")

7. Help the child learn to wait ("You will have a turn in five minutes.")

8. Break tasks down into manageable parts so that children can see how much progress they are making.

How To Provide An Environment Of Acceptance

This can be accomplished by adult behavior such as:

1. Showing respect for each child.

2. Listening and responding to children.

3. Showing affection and personal regard (greeting by name, one-to-one contact).

4. Giving attention to what the child considers important (looking at a block structure, locating a lost mitten).

5. Expressing appreciation, recognizing effort and accomplishments of each child, following through on promises.

6. Respecting and protecting individual rights and personal belongings (a "cubby" or box for storage, name printed on work in large, clear letters).

7. Acknowledging and accepting unique qualities of each child.

8. Avoiding situations which stereotype sex roles or racial/ ethnic backgrounds.

9. Providing ample opportunity for each child to experience success, to earn praise, to develop an "I can," "Let me try," attitude.

10. Accepting each child's language, whether it be standard English, a dialect or a foreign language, and fostering the child's comfort in using the primary language.

11. Providing opportunities to talk about feelings, to share responsibilities, to share humor.

How To Develop Intellectual Skills

Intellectual skills can be enhanced by providing a learning climate in which staff guide children to foster cognitive functioning (i.e., understanding, reasoning, conceptualizing, etc.)

How To Encourage Children To Solve Problems

Provide materials and time appropriate to the child's age and level of development in the areas of science, concepts of size, shape, texture, weight, color, etc., dramatic play, art, music, numerical concepts, spatial, locational and other relationships.

How To Promote Language Understanding

Some examples are:

1. Give children ample time to talk to each other and ask questions in the language of their choice.

2. Encourage free discussion and conversation between children and adults.

3. Provide games, songs, stories, and poems which offer new and interesting vocabulary.

4. Encourage children to tell and listen to stories.

How To Work Toward Recognition Of The Symbols For Letters and Numbers

Make use of information that is relevant to the child's interests, such as his name, telephone number, address and age. Make ample use of written language within the context of the child's understanding. For example, experience personal stories, make name labels and discuss signs that are familiar.

How To Encourage Children To Organize Their Experiences And Understand Concepts

The sequence of classroom activities should progress from simple to more complex tasks, and from concrete to abstract concepts. Activities can be organized around concepts to be learned.

How To Provide A Balanced Program

Although each day's activities should be planned by the staff, the schedule should allow ample time for both spontaneous activity by children and blocks of time for teacher-directed activities.

How To Promote Physical Growth

This can be accomplished through regular periods for physical activity (both indoor and out).

How To Provide Appropriate Guidance While Children Are Using Equipment And Materials

Staff should be actively involved with children during periods of physical activity. During such activities, staff should take opportunities to increase their contact with individual children. To ensure safety, activities should be adequately supervised.

How To Have A Curriculum Which Is Relevant

This can be accomplished by including in each classroom materials and activities which reflect the cultural background of the children. Examples of materials include: books, records, posters, maps, charts, dolls, clothing. Activities may include: celebration of cultural events and holidays, serving foods related to other cultures, stories, music, and games representative of children's background, and inviting persons who speak the child's native language to assist with activities.

How To Include Parents

Parents can be valuable resources in planning activities which reflect the children's heritage. Teachers may request suggestions from parents on ways to integrate cultural activities into the program. For example, parents may wish to: plan holiday celebrations, prepare foods unique to various cultures, recommend books, records or other materials for the classroom, act as classroom volunteers, suggest games, songs and art projects which reflect cultural customs.

How To Provide Health Education For Children

Activities to integrate educational aspects of other components into the daily education program could include: time to talk about physical and dental examinations in order to increase understanding and reduce fears, books and pictures about

doctors and dentists, materials for dramatic play (stethoscope, nurse's uniform, flashlight), role playing before and after visits to doctors, dentists, hospitals, clinics, etc., assistance in meal preparation, setting table, learning experiences through food preparation (adding liquids to solids, seasoning, freezing, melting, heating, cooling, cooking simple foods), books, picture, films, trips related to the source of foods (farm, garden, warehouse, market, grocery store.)

How To Provide Enhanced Understanding Between Parents and Staff

The plan should indicate some of the ways parents and staff will work together to understand each child and provide for his learning experiences. The plan should include details of ways the home and center will attempt to supplement each other in providing positive experiences for the child. Procedures should be established to facilitate maximum communication between staff and parents. Examples: newsletters, parent/teacher conferences, group meetings, phone calls, home visits, posters, bulletin boards, radio/TV announcements, orientation and training sessions, designing activities for children at home. Have the parent participate in classroom/center activities. Also provide parents with workshops, publications, and special referrals, etc.

(This section is reprinted with permission (1987) from Head Start Performance Standards, Department of Health and Human Services, Publication OHDS 84-31131)

49

PART NINE: <u>CHILD SAFETY</u>

Safety First!

1. Indoor and outdoor space should be sufficient and appropriate for necessary program activities and for support functions. (offices, food preparation, custodial services if they are conducted on the premises.) In addition, rest/nap facilities and space for isolation of sick children should be available.

2. Radiators, stoves, hot water pipes, portable heating units, and similar potential hazards are adequately screened or insulated to prevent burns.

3. No highly flammable furnishings or decorations shall be used.

4. Flammable and other dangerous materials and potential poisons shall be stored in locked cabinets or storage facilities accessible only to authorized persons. Cleaning supplies and potentially dangerous materials should be stored separately from food and out of reach of children.

5. Emergency lighting shall be available in case of power failure. High powered flashlights may be used. Candles are fire hazards.

6. Approved, working fire extinguishers shall be readily available. Adults in the program should be able to locate and properly operate fire extinguishers.

7. Indoor and outdoor premises shall be kept clean and free, on a daily basis, of undesirable and hazardous material and conditions. If evidence of rodents or vermin is found, the local health or sanitation department may provide assistance or referral for exterminators. At regular intervals, programs should be checked for and correct splintered surfaces, extremely sharp or protruding corners, or edges, loose or broken parts. All clear glass doors should be clearly marked with opaque tape to avoid accidents.

8. Outdoor play areas shall be made so as to prevent children from leaving the premises and getting into unsafe and unsupervised areas. Where outdoor space borders on unsafe areas (traffic, streets, ponds, swimming areas) adults should always be positioned to supervise the children. If possible, such areas should be enclosed.

9. Paint coatings on premises used for care of children shall be determined to assure the absence of a hazardous quantity of lead. Old buildings may be dangerous. Be sure to check for lead contamination. The local public health department can be contacted to provide information on lead poisoning and to detect hazardous quantities of lead in the facility.

10. Rooms shall be well lighted. Fixtures which have a low

glare surface to sufficiently diffuse and reflect light may be useful. Use bulbs with sufficient wattage. Check and replace burned-out bulbs regularly.

11. A source of water approved by the appropriate local authority shall be available in the facility. Adequate toilets and handwashing facilities shall be available and easily reached by children. Verify state and local licensing requirements in these areas.

12. All sewage and liquid waste shall be disposed of through a sewer system approved by an appropriate responsible authority, and garbage and trash shall be stored in a safe and sanitary manner until collected. Disposal problems can be referred to the local sanitation and public work department. Keep all waste materials away from children's activity areas and from areas used for storage and for preparation of food.

13. There shall be at least 35 square feet of indoor space per child available for the care of children (i.e., exclusive of bathrooms, halls, kitchen, and storage places). There shall be at least 75 square feet per child outdoors. (This space regulation varies from state to state. Check with your own regulatory agency) Where minimum space is not available, various alternatives can be considered. For example, a variation in program design could be to stagger the program day, the program week, and outdoor play periods. In this manner, all children will not be present at the same time. In some cases, outdoor space requirements may be met by arranging for daily use of an adjoining or nearby school yard, park, playground, vacant lot, or other space. Be sure that these areas are easily accessible and fulfill the necessary safety requirements. In some cases, it may be necessary to locate more suitable facilities.

14. Adequate provisions shall be made for handicapped children to ensure their safety and comfort. Ramps, railings, and special materials and equipment may be needed in order to allow such children maximum possible mobility. Community resources may be used to acquire needed special materials and services. **Confirm compliance with all state and local licensing requirements.**

(This section is reprinted with permission (1987) from Head Start Performance Standards, Department of Health and Human Services, Publication OHDS 84-31131)

52

PART TEN: <u>CLASSROOM SPACE PLANNING</u>

What Are The Recommended Centers For Learning?

Classroom Furniture

It is important that children work and play in a room that is attractive, orderly, and functional. Adequate storage and display units, lockers, screens, tables and chairs are essential. This is an action area where space is vital and room arrangements must shift and change to accommodate new activities. Classroom furniture should be flexible, easy to move, safe, sturdy and "childsized."

Each child should have an individual cubby or locker space. Separate compartments for coats and personal possessions help children to learn to take care of their belongings and develop a sense of independence and responsibility. These lockers should be placed where they are easily accessible but do not interfere with classroom activities.

Tables should be large enough to provide ample work space. They can be combined or moved to suit the activity.

Storage cabinets should have open shelves that are sufficiently low to enable children to select and put away their own materials. They should be accessible to the areas they serve. The book display unit should be at the proper height for children and low enough to allow the teacher to observe the activities.

Young children need a chance to relax and slow down during their busy day. Cots or mats give children a chance to rest comfortably. They can be stacked and stored conveniently in an out-of-the-way spot.

Active Play

Growing children need many opportunities to engage in large muscle activities. They delight in climbing, lifting, pushing, pulling. They are developing skills of balance and coordination. Through active play, children build confidence in their motor ability, learn to solve problems, explore on their own, and enjoy the companionship of their peers.

It is recommended that the active play area be safely enclosed, and large enough to provide for a variety of activities. Play equipment should be selected for safety and durability. It should lend itself to a variety of creativeness and draw ideas for play from the children. There should be suffcient play material to offer a wide range of experiences and allow all children to participate freely.

The outdoor environment should be arranged to offer opportunities to explore, discover and experiment. The play equipment should be placed so that activities do not interfere with one another and so that children's activities can be easily observed.

Block Play

Blocks are the most important play material in Kindergarten and preschool. Block play contributes greatly to the physical, social, emotional and intellectual growth of young children. It provides opportunities for manipulation and coordination. It aids the development of initiative and independence, creative expression and imagination. Block building helps to clarify ideas

through home and community life structures. It leads to cooperative play and encourages language development. Basic mathematical concepts are developed as children explore the relationship of unit block sizes and shapes.

The block area should be located where there is adequate floor space for building, away from the path of other activities. Low, open-shelved block cabinets should be provided so that children can reach the blocks easily and put them back by shape and size. Teaching children the proper method of storing blocks is essential to their learning to be neat and orderly in all areas of the classroom. Unit blocks should be of durable hardwood with all edges beveled to prevent splintering and wear at the corners. Smooth sanded surfaces and precise dimensions are important for safe handling and effective building. A good variety of block accessories is essential. With a selection of vehicles, farm and zoo animals, block people and colored cubes, children can project themselves imaginatively into block activity.

Dramatic Play

Dramatic play helps the child to come to terms with the world. The Housekeeping corner is one of the most important centers for such play. Children can try on self and family roles, work out their problems and concerns and act out familiar situations.

The Housekeeping Center should be a defined area, perhaps using low shelves or screens as boundaries. There should be ample room for children to move freely as they play. Furnishings should be arranged to suggest a home environment. The equipment should be sturdy, child-sized, realistic in design, and easy to clean. In addition to the basic furniture, there should be sufficient accessory material to stimulate a child's imagination. Dishes, telephones, play foods, cooking utensils, dolls, and dressup clothes add a realistic touch.

Wood-Working

Working with wood is an appealing and rewarding experience. Boys and girls become involved with action and react to the sound as they learn to saw or to hammer a nail in straight. The opportunities for creative expression, large muscle building, and continuing practice in eye-hand coordination are many.

Effective wood-working requires a sturdy workbench, real tools of good quality and an assortment of soft wood. The workbench should be placed where it can be well supervised. The tools should be placed where they are accessible and easy to keep in order. Lumber yards and carpentry shops are good sources for wood scraps. Safety goggles should be worn at all times in the wood-working area.

Creative Art

Children can express their feelings, ideas, and interest through creative art experiences. They learn to rely on their personal taste and judgment and take pride in their own efforts. Art activities help develop coordination, manipulative skills and aesthetic awareness.

Children need to work with different materials to explore the properties and possibilities of each. Clay, crayons, papers,

chalk, paste and collage materials should be kept on low, open shelves near the tables so that children can select and return them easily. Scissors should be in a rack or safe storage. For convenience, clay can be formed into handful-sized balls ahead of time covered with a damp cloth and stored in an air-tight container.

Painting at the easel is an important art experience. Easels should be adjustable, easy to clean and large enough to permit free arm movements. The easel should be placed near a good source of light and, if possible, near a sink where children can wash their hands and clean the brushes.

Rhythm, Music, and Sound

Music is one other most natural and spontaneous activities for young children. There should be time in their day to sing, to listen to music, to experiment with tone and sound, to use their bodies in rhythmic movement.

A phonograph and records, rhythmic and tonal instruments and an autoharp or piano are important elements of music activity. Several instruments placed on a shelf, or perhaps taken outside on special days, give children a chance to experiment with sound and create rhythmic patterns of their own. An easy-to-operate durable phonograph located in a quiet corner provides listening enjoyment and gives a feeling of responsibility and independence. The open space required for movement to music and rhythms can be easily provided by pushing aside table and chairs.

Classroom Library

Children develop an awareness of the joy of reading through book and story experiences. Books provide pleasure and information.

Children need a quiet corner where they can enjoy the classroom book. A good selection on a low bookcase encourages looking and choosing. A round table and chairs and a comfortable rocker will invite children to relax and "read" a favorite story.

The classroom library should include children's classics and the best of current books. There should be books of rhyme, books of fantasy and imagination and books that give information. Books should be added periodically during the year to spark new interests.

Relationships, Small Muscle Activities, Reading and Language Development, Number Readiness

Puzzles, manipulatives and construction toys give children opportunities to solve problems and gain confidence in their abilities. As they play, children strengthen coordination of eye and hand movements and further their ability to see that certain things go together. Many of these self-directive materials help the young children to see differences in size, shape and color. Others develop perception, judgment, creativity and a sense of design.

Children need concrete objects to count, games of matching, pictures to put in sequence, tactile letters and numbers to handle. With such tools, children can experiment, make discoveries and develop concepts without formalized instructions. Direction experiences with reading and number readiness materials establish a sound foundation for reading and mathematics.

56

Material for table activity should be placed on low shelves or in trays near the tables that will be used. Encouraging children to put away finished activities will help to prevent loss of parts and develop orderliness. There should be a sufficient variety of materials available to challenge children at varying stages of development.

Science

Young children are eager to understand the "whys" and "hows" of their environment. They need many opportunities to ask questions and to look for answers. Children make discoveries as they experiment with such materials as magnets, measuring cups and prisms. They learn more about their world as they examine a sea shell, watch a classroom pet or use a magnifying glass.

A counter top or table is a good place to display science materials. Room to spread out objects encourages experimentation. Natural science materials, that are rotated often, such as rocks, leaves, candles, or perhaps a handful of snow, can be gathered by the children and teacher. Plants, fish amd small pets are welcome additions. Other science materials and measuring devices should be provided for a rich program of discovery.

(Reprinted with permission of Child Craft Education Corporation, 20 Kilmer Road, Edison, NJ 08818)

Equipment and Supplies

Before purchasing any equipment and/or supplies, evaluate the safety considerations. Although the toy may appear safe, it may not be safe or appropriate for all age groups.

Betty Jo Marshall and Irene Hoogenboom, Educational Specialists at ENVIRONMENTS, INC. have generously shared their recommended equipment and materials list. You may use this as a guide for a classroom of up to twenty five children (3-5 year olds). If you have questions or would like free planning assistance, you may call them at 1-800-EI-CHILD, or write Environments, Inc., P.O. Box 1348, Beaufort, SC 29901.

The Early Years Room:

2 - 30" x 60" Tables
1 - Round Table
17 - 12" Chairs
2 - 17" Chairs
2 - Hinged Storage Units
1 - Storage Shelf Unit
Assorted Storage Trays and Bins
1 - Bulletin Board Screen
1 - Set/2 Child's Rockers
25 - Rest Cots (or Mats)
1 - Classroom Record Player

1 - 24" x 48" Table
1 - Group Table
8 - 10" Chairs
5 - Locker Units
2 - Storage Cabinets
1 - Book Display Unit
1 - Utility Cart
2 - Pegboard Screens
1 - Adult Rocking Chair
1 - A-V Cabinet
1 - Listening Center Set

Gross Motor Skills:

1 - Action Environment
2 - Nesting Bridges
2 - 12" Institutional Trikes
1 - 14" Institutional Trike
2 - 6" Playground Balls

1 - Gangway Ladder
1 - Log Cabin with Floor
2 - Supercycles
4 - 8 1/2" Playground Balls
1 - Hand Pump

Social Concepts:

1 - Acrylic Mirror
1 - Set of 4 Kitchen Units
1 - Hat Set
2 - Sets of 2 Chairs
1 - Housekeeping Stand
1 - Big Baby, Black
1 - Eve Girl Doll
10 - Small World Dolls
1 - Doll Bed
1 - Indestructible Dishes
1 - Doll Blanket Set
1 - Cultural USA Puzzle
1 - Folding Pretend Screen Bar
1 - Set of Fruit
1 - Produce Set
1 - Double Telephone Booth
1 - Strangers

1 - Dress-up Tree
1 - Vanity Set with Chair
1 - Wooden Round Table
1 - Housecleaning Set
1 - Big Baby, White
1 - Adam Boy Doll
1 - Big Baby Doll Clothes
1 - Bentwood Doll Carriage
1 - Stir & Bake Set
1 - Chest of Drawers
1 - Children of the World
1 - Large Cash Register
1 - Play Money Set
1 - Set of Vegetables
1 - Food Set
1 - Survival Signs
1 - My Body is Private

1 - I've Got Super Power
1 - Home/Community Helpers
1 - Children & the Law
1 - My Community

Creative Expression:

2 - Adjustable Double Easels
1 - Paint Drying Rack
1 - Preschool Easel Brushes
2 - Sets of 5 Chubby Brushes
1 - Dozen No-Spill Paint Cups
1 - Case/White Drawing Paper
1 - Plasticolor Class Pack
1 - Play-Doh Class Assortment
3 - Dozen Boxes-Large Crayons
1 - Bag of 50 Pencil Grips
2 - Six 8 oz. Bottles/Glue
2 - Sets/50 Paint Spreaders
2 - Teacher's Shears
1 - Case/Fingerpaint Paper
1 - Case of Newsprint
1 - Case/White Drawing Paper
2 - Case/ruled Newsprint
3 - Set/Powder Paint Assortment
4 - Yellow Finger Paint
1 - Sand and Water Table
1 - Sand Play Set
1 - Sand Tools Set
1 - Waterpump
15-20 - Asst. Children's Records
6 - Smocks
1 - Set of 4 Play Trays
2 - Mess Mats
1 - Cookie Cutting Set
1 - Clay Hammer
1 - Cases of Modeling Clay
2 - Dumpty Crayons
2 - Dozen Sets Markers
1 - Box/144 Jumbo Pencils
1 - Glitter Set
2 - Six Pint Jars/Paste
2 - Dozen Safety Scissors
1 - Scissors Rack
1 - Case of Art Tissue
2 - Case/12" x 18" Manila
1 - Roll of Butcher Paper
2 - Set/Construction Paper
4 - Red Finger Paint
4 - Blue Finger Paint
1 - Sand/Water Utensils Set
1 - Sand Shapes
1 - Sand Mill
1 - Water Transport
25 - Player Rhythm Set

Blocks and Accessories:

1 - Half Kindergarten Block Set
1 - Large Wild Animals
1 - Wild Kingdom
1 - Trees of the Forest
1 - Farm Friends
1 - Black Family Group
1 - Colorful Cars
1 - Small Vinyl Vehicles
6 - Land, Sea, Air Vehicles
1 - Mini Traffic Signs
3 - Heavy-Duty Vehicles
1 - Ride-On Wooden Bus
2 - Cardboard Blocks Set
1 - Giant Wild Animals
1 - Barnyard Animals Set
1 - Story Book City
1 - Wooden Play Figures
1 - White Family Group
1 - Career Figures Set
1 - Speedster Set
1 - Midget Fleet
1 - Wooden Traffic Signs
7 - Mid-Size Vehicles
1 - Earth Hauler
1 - Cargo to Go

Fine Motor Skills:

1 - Mobilo Class Set
1 - Easy Grip Pegs
1 - Large Beads & Laces
1 - Large Lego Basic Set
1 - Large Lego Building Plates
1 - Set of 4 Dressing Pads
1 - Jumbo Tactilmat Pegboard
1 - Lacing Shapes
1 - Threading Spools
1 - Lacing Disks
1 - Lacing Slip-On-Shoe
1 - See Me Lock Box

1 - Dr. Drew's Blocks
1 - Bill Ding & Friends
6 - Small Duplo Plates
1 - Large Duplo Building Plate
1 - Duplo Farm Set
1 - Duplo Animals & Fencing
1 - Duplo Vehicles
1 - Duplo Community Figures
1 - Beads & Baubles
1 - Bristle Blocks
4 - 10" Wooden Pegboard
1 - Pipe Construction

1 - Colored Blocks
1 - Klondikers
1 - Large Duplo Basic Set
1 - Duplo Harbor Set
1 - Duplo Home Environment
1 - Duplo Family Figures
1 - Lego People
1 - Triangle Blocks
1 - Ji-Gan-Tiks
1 - Set of 1000 Pegs
1 - Create-It

Basic Concepts:

3 - Wooden Puzzle Racks
1 - Preschool Puzzle Set
1 - Jumbo Playboard
1 - Shape Standard
1 - Fit-A-Space
1 - Large Attribute Blocks
1 - Disney Puzzle Set
4 - Large Duplo Building Plates
1 - Lady Bug Knobbed Puzzle
1 - Rainbow Knobbed Puzzle
1 - Thanksgiving Puzzle
1 - Rainbow Pie
1 - Shape Sorting Board
1 - Relationchips
1 - Wooden Sorting Figures
1 - Dino-Sort
1 - Colorama
1 - Kitty Kat Color Bingo
1 - Duplo Domestic Animals
1 - Sorting Box Combination
1 - Beginning Geometric Shapes
1 - Set/6 Difference Puzzles
1 - Wooden Animal Dominoes

1 - Beginners' Puzzle Set
1 - Building Beakers
1 - Circle Sorter
1 - Montessori Stencils
1 - Teddy Bear Bingo
1 - Animal Shapes
1 - Fit-In Perception Set
1 - Geometric Match & Count
1 - Cat Knobbed Puzzle
1 - Jack-O-Lantern Puzzle
1 - Teddy Bear Counters
1 - Knobbed Shapes Puzzle
1 - Link & Learn
1 - Count & Sort Set
2 - Count & Sort Trays
1 - Counter Bowls
1 - Stacking Trays
1 - Duplo Mosaics
1 - Jumbo Parquetry Blocks
1 - Butterfly Tiles
1 - Texture Boards
1 - Tri-3 Game
1 - Differix

Language Arts:

1 - Basic Book Set
1 - Flannel Board Story Kit
1 - Capital Flannel Letters
1 - Lower Case Flannel Letters
1 - Plush Puppets Set 2
1 - White Family Puppets
1 - Community Workers Puppets
1 - Simple See-Quees
1 - Building a Snowman
1 - Go-Together Matchmates
1 - Kids of World Wall Cards
1 - Kitty/Kat Alphabet Bingo
1 - Manuscript Wall Cards

1 - Preschool Book Set
1 - Disney Flannel Asst.
1 - Flannel Board
1 - Plush Puppets Set 1
3 - Puppet Storage Stands
1 - Black Family Puppets
1 - Eensy Weensy Spider
1 - Science See-Quees
1 - Eating an Apple
1 - ABC & Number Turtle
1 - Alpha Dragon
1 - GOAL Kit - Level 1

PART ELEVEN: SELECTED RESOURCES

Selected Resources

This resource list is "current" as of this printing. Oftentimes, books, pamphlets and referral information become dated and are no longer offered.

Non-Profit Child Care Association: The Child Care Information Service of the National Association For the Education Of Young Children (CCIS/NAEYC) is a centralized source of referrals and resources on national child care issues. Some of the available information includes statistics, licensing provisions, referrals to experts and organizations, publications, program information, etc. Call 1-800-424-2460 whenever you run into a problem. (They are a non-profit organization and a clearing house for early childhood information).

Publications

*Child Care Initiatives for Working Parents: Why Employers Get Involved, R.Y. Magid (1983). American Management Associations, 135 W. 50th Street, New York, NY 10020 ($13.50)
Reports results of survey on use and sponsorship of child care, identifies new directions and benefits for employers, and reviews economic considerations.

*Child Care and the Working Parent: First Steps Toward Employer Involvement in Child Care, B. Adolf & K. Rose (1982). Children at Work, 569 Lexington Avenue, New York, NY 10022. 212-758-7428, ext. 239 ($15.00)
Basic information needed to involve employers in options for providing child care. Includes formal and informal needs assessments.

*Employed Parents and Their Children: A Data Book (1982), Children's Defense Fund, 122 C Street, N.W., Washington, D.C. 20001. 202-628-8787 ($9.00)
Summarizes data useful in planning policies and programs to serve working parents and their children.

*Employer Supported Child Care: Investing in Human Resources, S. Burud, P. Aschbacher, & J. McCroskey (1984). Auburn House, 131 Clarendon Street, Boston, MA 02116. 617-247-2650 ($26.95 hardcover, $17.00 paper)
Offers guidelines and models for employers interested in child care. Includes details for conducting needs assessment.

*Encouraging Employer Support to Working Parents: Community Strategies for Change, D. Friedman (1983). Center for Public Advocacy Research, 12 W. 37th Street, New York, NY 10018. 212-564-9220 ($9.00)
Trends in employer-supported child care.

*Child Care Employee Project, P.O. Box 5603, Berkeley, CA 94705.
415-653-9889
    This resource organization offers a newsletter, materials,
and technical assistance designed to improve child care working
conditions. Topics include substitute employees and coffee break
policies, grievance procedures, occupational health and safety,
employment rights, staff relations, working with boards of
directors, unionizing, and staff evaluations.

*Day Care Information Service Newsletter, 4550 Montgomery Avenue,
Suite 700 North, Bethesda, MD 20814-3382. 301-656-6666
    Monthly newsletter with latest information about food
program, insurance, dependent care program, day care hotline, and
other day care resources. Subscription available.

*Child Care Information Exchange, R. Neugebauer, ed., P.O. Box
2890, Redmond, WA 98052. 206-882-1066. (subscription $20 a year)
    Excellent bimonthly management magazine for administrators of
child care programs.

*Management of Child Development Centers, V. Hildebrand (1984).
McMillan, Front and Brown Streets, Riverside, NJ 08075.
212-702-2000 ($24.00)
    Offers management principles regarding finances, space
management, curriculum, health, staff, parents, and other aspects
of programs for young children.

*Fundraising for Early Childhood Programs: Getting Started and
Getting Results, M. Finn (1982). NAEYC, 1834 Connecticut Avenue,
N.W., Washington, D.C. 20009 ($3.85)
    Complete guide to seeking financial support for early
childhood programs.

*Managing the Day Care Dollars: A Financial Handbook, G.G. Morgan
(1982). Gryphon House, 3706 Otis Street, P.O. Box 217, Mt.
Rainier, MD 20822 ($8.70)
    Complete handbook for financial planning and management with
emphasis on policy and high quality care.

*Centers of Disease Control, Virginia Spears, Center for
Professional Development and Training, 1600 Clifton Road,
Atlanta, GA 30333. 404-262-6681
    The CDC is developing recommendations for child care staff to
control the spread of infectious disease. A training packet
including posters, letters to parents, and background
information will soon be offered.

*American Academy of Pediatrics, P.O. Box 1034, 1801 Hinman
Avenue, Evanston, IL 60204. 312-869-4255
    The AAP expects to release guidelines for health in child
care. Call or write for a list of other resources on various
child health topics.

*Caring for Infants and Toddlers: What Works, What Doesn't, Vol. 2, R. Lurtie & R. Neugebauer, eds. (1982). Child Care Information Exchange, P.O. Box 2890, Redmond, WA 98052 ($10.00)
    Discusses curriculum, health, parents, environment, staff, and administration of programs for infants and toddlers.

*The Infants We Care For, L. Dittmann, ed. (1984). NAEYC, 1834 Connecticut Avenue, N.W., Washington, D.C. 20009. 800-424-2460 ($3.85)
    Practical considerations for operating home or center-based infant care programs. Topics include staff selection and training, budgeting, facility equipment and program planning.

*The Toddler Center: A Practical Guide To Day Care for One-and-Two-Year-Olds, M. O'Brien, J. Porterfield, E. Herbert-Jackson, & T.R. Risley (1979). University Park Press, 300 N. Charles Street, Baltimore, MD 21201. 301-547-0700 ($19.95)
    Practical guide to design management, and operation of group care for toddlers.

*Planning Environments for Young Children: Physical Space, S. Kritchevsky & E. Prescott (1977). NAEYC, 1834 Connecticut Avenue, N.W., Washington, D.C. 20009. 202-232-8777 or 800-424-2460 ($2.00)
    Relates program goals to use of indoor and outdoor space. Suggests ways to arrange equipment and plan play areas.

*Quality Day Care: A Handbook of Choices for Parents and Caregivers, R.C. Endsley & M.R. Bradbard (1981). Prentice-Hall, P.O. Box 500, Englewood Cliffs, NJ 07632. 201-592-2637 ($7.45)
    Reviews child care trends, aspects of good quality programs and procedures for selecting and monitoring child care.

*Activities for School-Age Child Care, R. Blau, E.H. Brady, I. Bucher, T. Hiteshew, A. Zavitkovsky (1977). NAEYC, 1834 Connecticut Avenue, N.W., Washington, D.C. 20009. 202-232-8777 or 800-424-2460 ($3.85)
    Guide for planning crafts, dramatic play, and other ideas in working with school-age children.

*School-Age Child Care: An Action Manual, R.K. Baden, A. Genser, J.A. Levine, M. Seligson, Auburn House, 131 Clarendon Street, Boston, MA 02116. 617-247-2650 ($14.95)
    Comprehensive guide for starting and managing a program serving school-age children. Includes sample forms.

*Child Care Law Center, 625 Market Street, Suite 816, San Francisco, CA 94105. 415-495-5498
    Offers more than 50 brief and inexpensive publications dealing with legal issues such as zoning, child abuse, liability, and taxes. Request complete list of titles.

*Nursery School and Day Care Management Guide, C. Cherry (1978). David S. Lake Publishers, 19 Davis Drive, Belmont, CA 94002
    Great book to help you with many aspects of setting up a program.

*Pre-K Today, Scholastic, Inc., 730 Broadway, New York, NY 10003
    Published eight times a year. It is filled with ideas for teaching and caring for infants to five year olds. Subscription available.

*Day Care Parenting, A. Hubbard & C. Hayburn, Four Seasons Publications, Box 125, Newark, DE 19715-0125 ($4.95)
    This handbook is a great bargain! It provides a concise, accurate picture of quality day care. It could be used for ideas for your parent handbook or for workshop ideas.

Resource Groups

American Montessori Society, 150 Fifth Avenue, Suite 203, New York, NY 10011. 212-924-3209

Catalyst, 14 East 60th Street, New York, NY 10022. 212-759-9700

Association for Childhood Education International, 11141 Georgia Avenue, Suite 200, Wheaton, MD 20902. 301-942-2443

The Conference Board, 845 Third Avenue, New York, NY 10022. 212-759-0900, ext. 371

Association Montessori International/USA, Houston Service Center, 11230 Harwin Drive, Houston, TX 77072. 713-879-1818

CDA National Credentialing Program, 1341 G Street, N.W., #802 Washington, D.C. 20005

Women's Bureau, U.S. Department of Labor, Room S-3315, 200 Constitution Avenue, Washington, D.C. 20210. 212-523-6641

Child Care Employee Project, P.O. Box 5603, Berkeley, CA 94705. 415-653-9889

Child Care Information Service, 330 South Oak Knoll, Room 26, Pasadena, CA 91101. 818-796-4341

Center for Public Advocacy Research, 12 W. 37th Street, New York, NY 10018. 212-564-9220

Child Care Law Center, 625 Market Street, Suite 816, San Francisco, CA 94105. 415-495-5498

Child Care Support Center, P.O. Box 791, Boulder, CO 80306. 303-441-3180

Children's Council of San Francisco, 3896 24th Street, San Francisco, CA 94164. 415-282-7858

The Work and Family Information Center, The Conference Board, 845 Third Avenue, New York, NY 10022. 212-759-0900
National Association for Child Care Management, 1800 M Street, N.W., Suite 1030N, Washington, D.C. 20036. 202-452-8100

National Black Child Development Institute, 1463 Rhode Island Avenue, N.W., Washington, D.C. 20005. 202-387-1281

National Employer Supported Child Care Project, P.O. Box 40652, Pasadena, CA 91104-7652. 213-796-4341

School-Age Child Care Project, Wellesley College Center for Research on Women, Wellesley, MA 02181. 617-431-1453

Southern Association On Children Under Six, P.O. Box 5403, Brady Station, Little Rock, AR 72215. 501-227-6404

American Education Research Association, 1230 17th Street, N.W., Washington, D.C. 20036. 202-223-9485

Children Defense Fund, 122 C Street, N.W., Washington, D.C. 20001. 202-628-8787 (relates to child care legislation issues)

Child Welfare League of America, 67 Irving Place, New York, NY 10003. 212-254-7410 (publishes "Child Welfare" focusing on day care services)

Society for Research in Child Development, Institute of Human Development, 1209 Tolman Hall, University of California, Berkeley, CA 94720. 415-642-6401

Day Care and Child Development Council of America, 1012 14th Street, N.W., Washington, D.C. 20005. (magazines: "Voice For Children" and "Family Day Care Provider")

Children's Foundation, 1420 New York Avenue, N.W., Washington, D.C. 20005 (Information on child care food programs. They also offer a publication for home-based providers called "Family Day Care Bulletin.")

Association for Childhood Educational International (ACEI), 3615 Wisconsin Avenue, N.W., Washington, D.C. 20016. (publishes "Childhood Education Journal")

ERIC (Educational Resource Information Center/Early Childhood Education), University of Illinois at Urbana-Champaign, 805 W. Pennsylvania Avenue, Urbana, IL 61801

FREE Resource Materials

"Keeping Records In Small Business," and "Getting The Facts for Income" will help you with simple recordkeeping. Call 1-800-368-5855. This is a referral service for the Small Business Administration. They will give you all the information that you need for starting a business. If they can't help you they will refer you to the SBA office in a city near you. Also ask them for the telephone number of SCORE which is a free service provided by retired executives. Don't delay in calling them. It will be like having your own private consultant to answer your questions, all at no charge!

How To Facilitate Children's Problem Solving, by Elizabeth Crary. Send a S.A.S.E. to: Parenting Press, P.O. Box 15163, Seattle, WA 98115

New Creative Ideas For Early Childhood Classrooms, a free copy of the monthly publication, "In the Beginning" a thematic approach to early childhood education is available by sending your name, address, to Noah's Art, P.O. Box 513, Chanute, KS 66720

Crib Safety Tips, everything you always wanted to know about crib safety and more! Safe crib designs, accessories, mattresses, and hardware are all covered in the illustrated brochure, made available by the National Safety Council, PR Department B, 444 N,. Michigan Avenue, Chicago, IL 60611

Educational Activities, Inc., a free catalog of best selling early childhood recordings. Delightful songs keep children involved in learning basic skills through music and movement. Department PK, P.O. Box 392, Freeport, NY 11520

After School Resources Catalog, National newsletter on school age child care and 40 other resources and activity books. Write: Resources Catalog, School Age Notes, Box 120674, Nashville, TN 37212

Kimbo: The Children's Record Company, fun filled activity albums for infants and toddlers. "Get A Good Start," "A Thriller For Kids," "Baby Face." Send to: Free Catalog & Sampler record, Kimbo, P.O. Box 477-Z, Long Branch, NY 07740, 800-631-2187

Resources for Child Caring, Toys 'n Things Press, 906 N. Dale Street, St. Paul MN 55103. 800-423-8309. Call and ask for their free catalog.

"How to Choose A Good Early Childhood Program," and "How to Plan and Start A Good Early Childhood Program" (1983). NAEYC, 1834 Connecticut Avenue, N.W., Washington, D.C. 20009. 202-232-8777 or 800-424-2460. Single copies free with self-addressed, stamped business envelope.

Legal Handbook for Day Care Centers, L. Kotin, R.K. Crabtree, & W.F. Aikman (1981). Publication No. (OHDS) 83-30335. Allen Smith, Administration for Children, Youth and Families, U.S. Department of Health and Human Services, P.O. Box 1182, Washington, D.C. 20013. 202-755-7794. Comprehensive resource on legal aspects of establishing and operating a child care center.

ERIC Reports (Eric Document Reproduction Service), a public library can provide you with copies of articles written about day care, child care, child development, etc. These are usually copied from microfiche but are great reading. If they are unable to reprint at the library, they can give you ordering information. ERIC is a computerized library service for access to many documents prepared under government controls or grants. It is often the fastest way to obtain information on any subject related to early childhood.

Planning Space Requirements, Environments, Inc. are early childhood materials and equipment specialists. Call 1-800- EI-CHILD. They offer a free catalog which guides you in materials selection for opening a day care center grouped according to curriculum needs. They also will send you an 8 page book list and 5 pages of indexes to audio-visual and other resources. Call and ask for the recommended list for "Classroom & Playground Expansion" as well a "Planning Layouts."

Agricultural Extension Service, is an agency which puts out a number of excellent free publications on a variety of topics related to children. Be sure to call and ask to be placed on the mailing list. Also ask if you qualify for any milk or cheese subsidy program.

Additional Free Resources

Business Development Pamphlets, write a note or postcard to SBA. P.O. Box 15434, Ft. Worth, TX 76114 and request a list of these pamphlets. They discuss management techniques, problems and help the small business owner to look before leaping into a business.

Playground Safety, as of early 1987, two volumes were available free of charge from the U.S. Consumer Product Safety Commission, Washington, D.C. 20207. I would recommend that you send a postcard or brief letter requesting copies of Volume I: General Guidelines For New And Existing Playgrounds, and Volume II: Technical Guidelines For Equipment And Surfacing, 800-638-2772, 800-492-8363 (Maryland), or 800-638-8333 (Alaska, Hawaii, Puerto Rico, Virgin Islands)

Development of Day Care Centers, a series of day care books available at no charge from the U.S. Department of Health and Human Services. Written requests to: Ms. Rossie Kelly, Head Start Bureau, Department of Health and Human Services, P.O. Box 1182, Washington, D.C. 20013. This is a free offer that you do not want

to pass up! If they are no longer available from this agency, ask
where you can obtain copies of these invaluable guides.
202-755-7944

Connect Information Service, is an invaluable source of
information on early childhood development and constructive art
and play activities. In Pennsylvania, call 1-800-692-7288 and
explain the type of program that you offer. Ask them what free
publications and supplies are available. The "Preschool Package"
which is available at no charge will be a wonderful addition to
your teacher's library.

Child Safety Brochure, is a brochure of child care safety tips,
available free from Metropolitan Life Insurance, Inc., One
Madison Avenue, New York, NY 10010. Everything from child-
proofing - to play and toy safety is presented in a developmental
format covering infants to seven year olds.

GALLAGHER, JORDAN & ASSOC.

P.O. Box 555

Worcester, PA 19490

(215) 584-5304

Where Can I Obtain Free Supplies?

Listed below are some locations where I have obtained free arts and crafts supplies:

Wallpaper Store - old sample books
Paint Store - sample paint charts
Lumber Yard - scraps of wood (pine is preferable), pieces of
        lumber, use for building blocks
Carpet Store - floor samples
Fabric Store - spools, scraps, eyelet, ribbons, buttons
Tobacco Shop - cigar boxes
Printer - all sizes, shapes and texture paper
Garment Factory - pieces of fabric
Label Factory - stickers
Furniture & Appliance Store - large boxes
Farm Store - ice cream cartons
Computer Centers - printout paper
Cabinet Makers - wooden color samples
Medical Suppliers, Clinics, Drug Stores - tongue depressors and
        styrofoam
Grocery Stores, Liquor Stores, Shoe Stores, - boxes and
        containers
Post Office - end sheets of stamps. You can color the zip code
        man and on the blank ones, you can design your own stamp
Newspaper - end rolls
Electric Supply Store - thin wire
Bar or Restaurant - wine corks
Airlines - plastic cups
Architectural Firm - drafting paper
Billboard Companies - large sheets of colored paper
Bottling Companies - bottle caps
Container Companies - large sheets of cardboard
Contractors - building scraps, linoleum pieces, sawdust
Power Companies - telephone poles, spools
Candy Manufactures - cans and boxes
Moving Company - large boxes
Gift Shop - styrofoam packing pieces
Fast Food Outlets - plates, napkins, "freebies," empty sour cream
        containers, margarine containers, etc.
Tire Store - truck or tractor tires for climbing

What Parents Can Save

"One man's junk is another's treasure." No truer words were ever spoken especially with children. The odd items we throw away without thought can provide creative and pleasurable hours of activities for children. Ask the parents to keep a box or bag in a cabinet. Their child would probably be thrilled to issue reminders about that paper towel roll or the margarine container. It is another area of "school-life" that the child and parent can share.

Here's a mini-list. You are bound to think of other items you can use.

Margarine containers
Empty oatmeal containers
Baby food jars
Shirt cardboards
Paper rolls from paper towels
Toilet paper rolls
Pipe cleaners
Tin cans with plastic lids
Clean, old clothes
Spring clothes pins
Large boxes
Long shoelace
1/2 gallon milk containers
Old calendar
Old greeting cards
Ribbon, yarn
Pinecones
Large paint brushes
Masking tape
Hard white beans
Ping pong balls
Cotton balls

Plastic lids of all sizes
Old magazines and catalogs
Egg cartons
Light weight cardboard of any kind
Paper rolls from foil, plastic wrap
Junk mail
Brown paper bags
Frozen juice cans
Used paper cups
Straws
Shoe boxes
Heavy string
Paper plates
Construction paper
Wrapping paper scraps
Old toothbrushes
Tin foil
Old tractor tire
Corn kernels
Deck of cards (full or partial)
Fabric scraps

APPENDIX

ALABAMA
Department of Pensions and Security
64 N. Union Street
Montgomery, AL 36130

ALASKA
Department of Health and Social Services
Division of Social Services
Pouch H-05
Juneau, AK 99811

ARIZONA
Child Day Care Health Consultant
Arizona State Department of Health
Phoenix, AZ 85007

ARKANSAS
Day Care Specialist
Department of Human Services
P.O. Box 1437
Little Rock, AR 72203

CALIFORNIA
Department of Social Services
744 P Street
Mail Station 19-50
Sacramento, CA 95814

COLORADO
Department of Social Services
1575 Sherman Street
Denver, CO 80203

CONNECTICUT
Day Care Licensing
Department of Health
79 Elm Street
Hartford, CT 06115

DELAWARE
Chief, Day Care Licensing
Bureau of Child Development
P.O. Box 309
Wilmington, DE 19899

DISTRICT OF COLUMBIA
Department of Human Resources
Washington, D.C. 20003

FLORIDA
Department of Health and
    Rehabilitative Services
1317 Winewood Boulevard
Tallahasee, FL 32301

GEORGIA
Child Care Licensing Unit
618 Ponce de Leon Avenue
Atlanta, GA 30308

HAWAII
Department of Social Services
    and Housing
Day Care Licensing Unit
Public Welfare Division
Honolulu, HI 96813

IDAHO
Day Care Licensing
Department of Health and Welfare
Statehouse
Boise, ID 83720

ILLINOIS
Day Care Licensing
Department of Children and
    Family Services
1 North Old State Capitol Plaza
Springfield, IL 62706

INDIANA
Day Care Supervisor
Department of Public Welfare
141 S. Meridian Street, 6th floor
Indianapolis, IN 46225

IOWA
Day Care Supervisor
Department of Social Services
Lucas State Office Building
Des Moines, IA 50319

KANSAS
Day Care Supervisor
Department of Social and
    Rehabilitation Services
State Office Building
Topeka, KS 66612

KENTUCKY
Department of Human Resources
Bureau for Social Services
275 E. Main Street
Frankfort, KY 40621

LOUISIANA
Department of Health and Human
   Resources
P.O. Box 3767
Baton Rouge, LA 70821

MAINE
Department of Human Services
Statehouse
Augusta, ME 04333

MARYLAND
Child Day CAre Center Coordinator
Deparmtnet of Health and Mental
   Hygiene
201 W. Preston Street
Baltimore, MD 21202

MASSACHUSETTS
Office for Children
Director of Day Care Licensing
120 Boylston Street
Boston, MA 02116

MICHIGAN
Department of Social Services
300 S. Capitol Avenue
Lansing, MI 48926

MINNESOTA
Department of Public Welfare
Licensing Division
Centennial Office Building
St. Paul, MN 55155

MISSISSIPPI
Day Care Supervisor
Department of Family and
   Children's Services
P.O. Box 1700
Jackson, MS 39205

MISSOURI
Department of Social Services
Division of Family Servies
Broadway State Office Building
P.O. Box 88
Jefferson City, MO 65103

MONTANA
Social and Rehabilitation
   Services
P.O. Box 4210
Helena, MT 59601

NEBRASKA
Day Care Welfare Consultant
Department of Public Welfare
P.O. Box 95026
Lincoln, NE 68509

NEVADA
State Department of Health
Department of Human Resources
505 E. King Street
Carson City, NV 89710

NEW HAMPSHIRE
Day Care Licensing
Division of Welfare
Concord, NH 03301

NEW JERSEY
Division of Youth and Family
   Services
Bureau of Licensing
1 S. Montgomery Street, #400
Trenton, NJ 08625

NEW MEXICO
Child Care Licensing
725 St. Michael's Drive
P.O. Box 968
Santa Fe, NM 87503

NEW YORK
Department of Social Services
40 N. Pearl Street
Albany, NY 12243

NORTH CAROLINA
Office of Child Day Care Licensing
Department of Social Services
P.O. Box 10157
Raleigh, NC 17605

NORTH DAKOTA
Supervisor of Children and
Family Day Care Services
State Capitol Building, 15th floor
Bismarck, ND 58501

OHIO
Department of Public Welfare
Division of Social Services
30 E. Broad Street, 30th floor
Columbus, OH 43215

OKLAHOMA
Children's Day Care Services
State Department of Public Welfare
P.O. Box 25352
Oklahoma City, OK 73125

OREGON
Department of Human Resources
Children's Service Division
198 Commercial Street, S.E.
Salem, OR 97310

PENNSYLVANIA
Licensing Supervisor
Children and Youth
1514 N. Second Street
Harrisburg, PA 17102
Philadelphia Area: 1-800-346-2929

PUERTO RICO
Puerto Rico Department of Social Services
P.O. Box 11697
Santurce, Puerto Rico 00908

RHODE ISLAND
Department of Social and
   Rehabilitative Services
610 Mt. Pleasant
Providence, RI 02908

SOUTH CAROLINA
South Carolina Department of
   Social Services
P.O. Box 1520
Columbia, SC 29202

SOUTH DAKOTA
Department of Social Services
Illinois Street, Kneip Building
Pierre, SD 57501

TENNESSEE
Day Care Licensing
Department of Human Services
111 Seventh Avenue North
Nashville, TN 37203

TEXAS
State Department of Public
   Welfare
105 W. Riverside Drive
Austin, TX 78704

UTAH
Division of Family Services
150 W. North Temple, Rm 370
P.O. Box 2500
Salt Lake City, UT 84110

VERMONT
Department of Social and
   Rehabilitation Services
State Office Building
Montpelier, VT 05602

VIRGIN ISLANDS
Department of Social Welfare
P.O. Box 539, Charlotte Amalie
St. Thomas, Virgin Islands 00801

VIRGINIA
Division of Licensing
8007 Discovery Drive
Richmond, VA 23288

WASHINGTON
Bureau of Children's Services
Dept. of Social & Health Services
Mail Stop, OB-2, 41-D
Olympia, WA 98504

WEST VIRGINIA
Day Care Unit
State Department of Welfare
1900 Washington Street, E.
Charleston, WV 25305

WISCONSIN
Department of Health and Social Services
1 West Wilson Street, Room 384
Madison, WI 53702

WYOMING
Day Care Supervisor
Division of Public Assistance
State Office Building
Cheyenne, WY 82002

INDEX